VLSI Design

For B.E VI Semester ECE Branch

As per the Syllabus of Anna University, Chennai

(Regulation-2013)

Dr.M. Meenakumari

Associate Professor

SNS College of Engineering

Coimbatore

Published by

BONFRING®
Intellectual Integrity

VLSI Design

ISBN 978-93-86638-60-1

Author

Dr.M. Meenakumari

Bonfring

309, 2nd Floor, 5th Street Extension, Gandhipuram,

Coimbatore-641 012.

Tamilnadu, India.

E-mail: info@bonfring.org

Website: www.bonfring.org

Phone: 0422 4213231

Dedicated to My Father

Thiru.T.S.Mariappan

Preface

The Electronics industry has achieved a remarkable growth over the last three decades, mainly due to the rapid advances in VLSI integration technologies. VLSI chips are widely used in various applications like: Voice and Data Communication networks, Digital Signal Processing, Commercial Electronics, Automobiles and Medicine. This book is designed as per the syllabus of Anna University 2013 Regulation for sixth semester ECE students.

The book is organized in five chapters. The first chapter discusses about the basic principle of MOS transistor, Electrical properties and its modeling. The second chapter deals about CMOS implementation of combinational circuits. The third chapter details about CMOS implementation of Sequential circuits. The fourth chapter enumerates the design of basic building blocks of the ALU. The fifth chapter elaborates the implementation techniques of designs in FPGA. The Question bank, two mark Questions with answers and previous year Anna University Questions are useful to the students. This book is more students friendly and simple to secure marks and simultaneously improve the knowledge.

Acknowledgement

First and foremost, I would like to thank God Almighty for giving me the strength, Knowledge, ability and opportunity to write this book.

I would like to offer heartfelt thanks to my family members for providing incredible support and encouragement for writing this book.

My Gratitude to the Management for providing the support and motivation to publish the book .My whole hearted thanks to the Principal Dr.N.Suresh Kumar to publish this book.

I express my deep sense of gratefulness to the Publishing Advisor, Bonfring Publication for bringing this book within a short period of time.

Dr.M. Meenakumari

EC6601 VLSI Design   L T P C 3 0 0 3

OBJECTIVES:

- In this course, the MOS circuit realization of the various building blocks that is common to any microprocessor or digital VLSI circuit is studied.
- Architectural choices and performance tradeoffs involved in designing and realizing the circuits in CMOS technology are discussed.
- The main focus in this course is on the transistor circuit level design and realization for digital operation and the issues involved as well as the topics covered are quite distinct from those encountered in courses on CMOS Analog IC design.

UNIT I: MOS TRANSISTOR PRINCIPLE   9

NMOS and PMOS transistors, Process parameters for MOS and CMOS, Electrical properties of CMOS circuits and device modeling, Scaling principles and fundamental limits, CMOS inverter scaling, propagation delays, Stick diagram, Layout diagrams.

UNIT II: COMBINATIONAL LOGIC CIRCUITS   9

Examples of Combinational Logic Design, Elmore's constant, Pass transistor Logic, Transmission gates, static and dynamic CMOS design, Power dissipation – Low power design principles.

UNIT III: SEQUENTIAL LOGIC CIRCUITS   9

Static and Dynamic Latches and Registers, Timing issues, pipelines, clock strategies, Memory architecture and memory control circuits, Low power memory circuits, Synchronous and Asynchronous design.

UNIT IV: DESIGNING ARITHMETIC BUILDING BLOCKS   9

Data path circuits, Architectures for ripple carry adders, carry look ahead adders, High speed adders, accumulators, Multipliers, dividers, Barrel shifters, speed and area tradeoff.

UNIT V: IMPLEMENTATION STRATEGIES   9

Full custom and Semi custom design, Standard cell design and cell libraries, FPGA building block architectures, FPGA interconnect routing procedures.

<table>
<tr><td>Chapter</td><td style="text-align:center">Contents</td><td>Page No</td></tr>
</table>

CHAPTER 1

MOS TRANSISTOR PRINCIPLE

1.1. Introduction

MOS transistor is a majority carrier device, in which the current in a Channel between the source and drain is modulated by a voltage applied to the gate. In NMOS, the majority carriers are electrons in the channel (region immediately under the gate) and hence increases the conductivity of the channel.

The operation of a PMOS transistor is analogous to the NMOS transistor, with the exception that the majority carriers are holes and voltages are negative with respect to the substrate.

MOS transistors act as ideal switches. An ON transistor passes a finite amount of current depending on terminal voltages. The switching behavior of an MOS transistor is characterized by threshold voltage V_t. This is defined as the voltage at which an MOS device begins to conduct. For gate voltage less than a threshold value, the channel is cut-off, thus   causing a very low drain-to-source current.

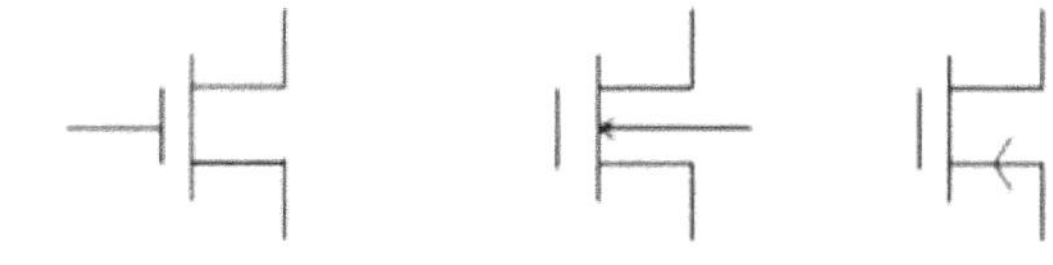

Figure 1.1: Symbol of NMOS

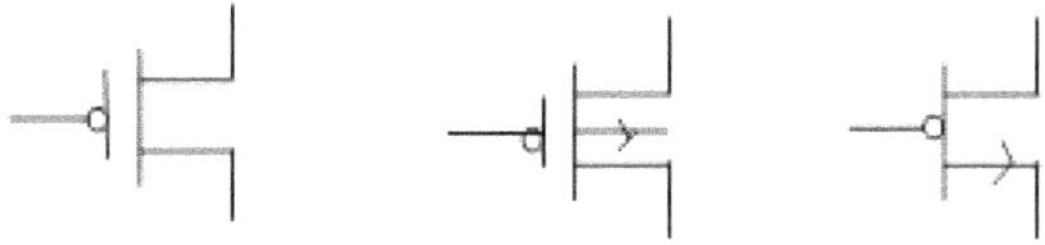

Figure 1.2: Symbol of PMOS

Enhancement Mode and Deletion Mode

The devices that are normally cut-off with zero gate bias are classified as enhancement mode devices, whereas those devices that conduct with zero gate bias are called depletion mode devices.

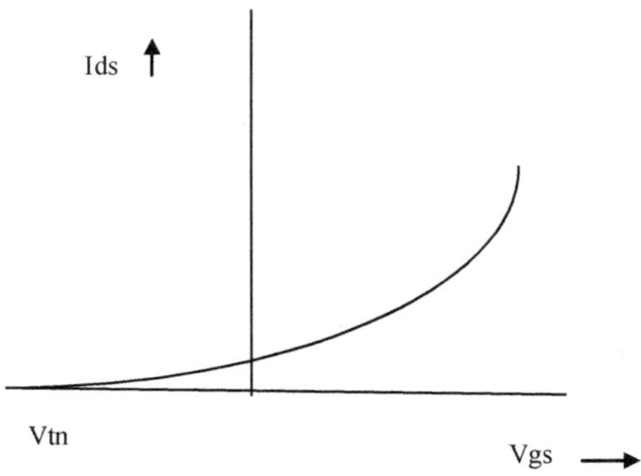

Figure 1.3: Characteristics of Depletion Mode NMOS

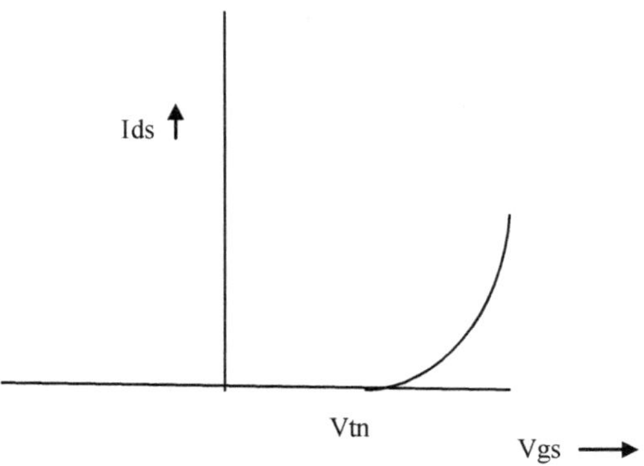

Figure 1.4: Characteristics of Enhancement Mode NMOS

PMOS Enhancement Mode

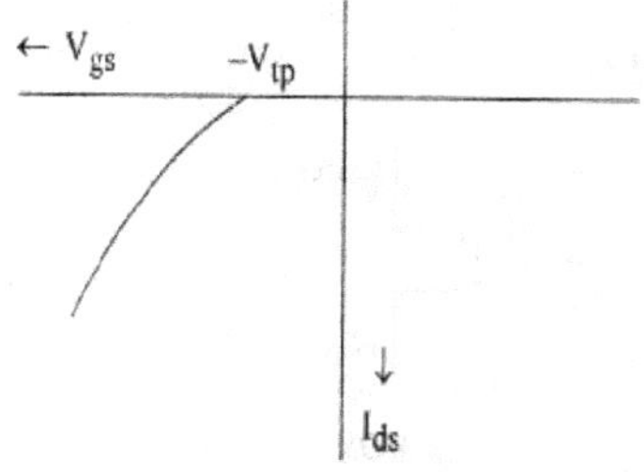

Figure 1.5: Characteristics of Enhancement Mode PMOS

Vgs = gate-to-source voltage

Ids = drain-to-source current

Vtp = Threshold voltage of a p-MOS transistor

If Vgs crosses Vtp then the device will conduct.

PMOS Depletion Mode

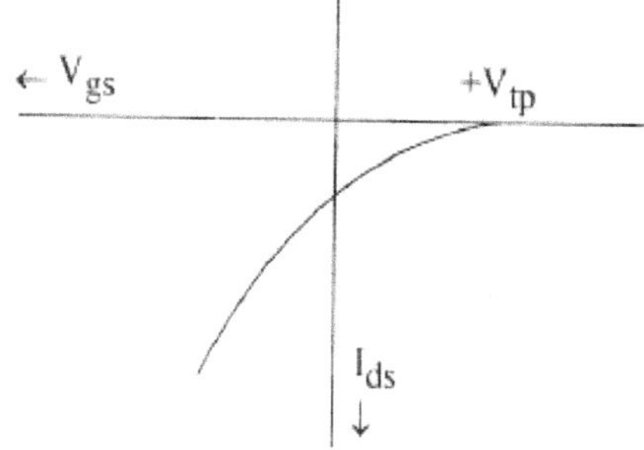

Figure 1.6: Characteristics of Depletion Mode PMOS

Vgs = gate-to-source voltage

Ids = drain-to-source current

Vtp = Threshold voltage of a p-MOS transistor

Even if Vgs = 0 the device will be conducting.

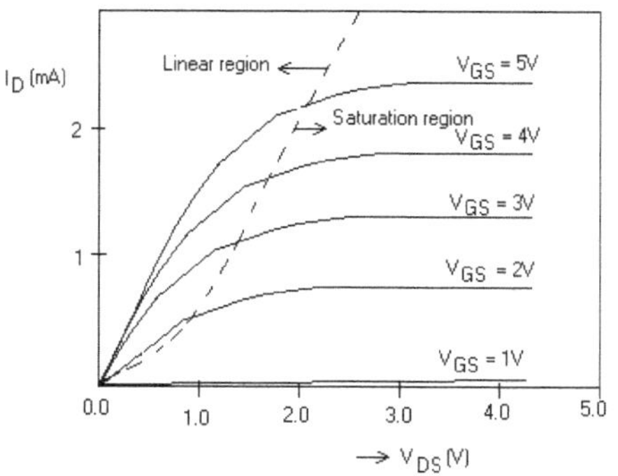

Figure 1.7: Drain Characteristics of NMOS Transistor

Threshold Voltage

Threshold Voltage V_t defines the voltage at which a MOS transistor begins to conduct. For voltages less than V_t the channel is cut off. Positive/negative voltage applied to the gate with respect to substrate enhances the number of electrons/holes in the channel and increases conductivity between source and drain.

Moore's Law

Gordon Moore founder of Intel Corporation made a prediction that number of transistors on a die will double for every 18 months. It implies the shrinking dimensions with constant rate of process improvement.

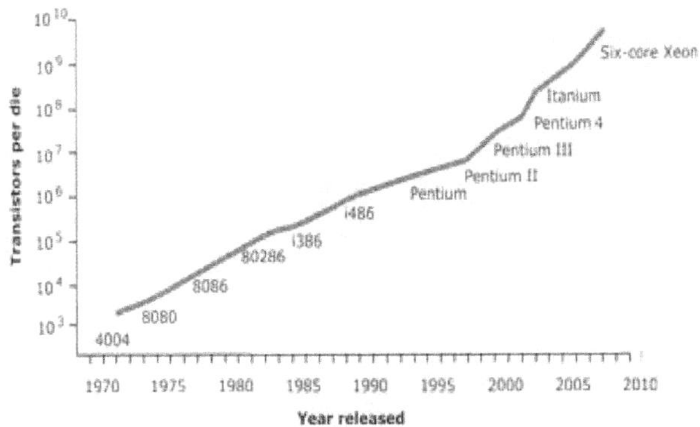

Figure 1.8: Moore's Law

1.2. NMOS Transistor Operation & Characteristics

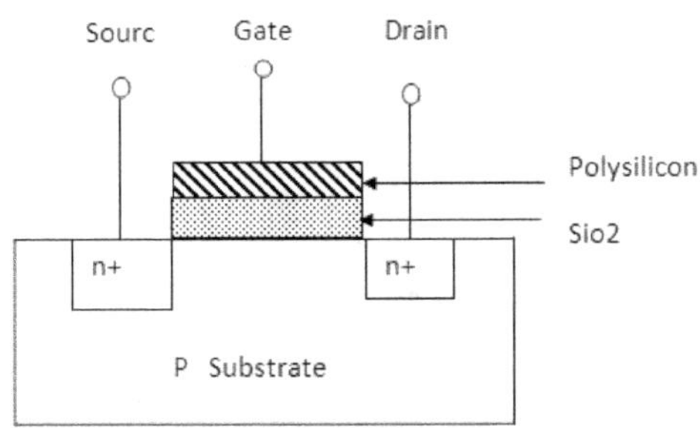

Figure 1.9: NMOS Transistor Structure

NMOS Enhancement

- When Vgs=0 & Vds =+ve , no current flows from source drain because source and drain are insulated from each other by two reverse biased PN junction.
- When +ve Vgs is applied to gate with respect to source & substrate produces an Electric field across the substrate which attracts electrons towards the gate and repels holes.

When Vgs is sufficiently large, the region under the gate changes from +ve to-ve because of accumulation of -ve charges. The surface of underlying p-type silicon is inverted. Vds is responsible for sweeping electrons in the channel from source towards drain. At source end of the channel full gate voltage is effective in inverting channel. At drain end, only the difference between gate and drain voltage is effective.

When effective gate voltage Vgs-vt > Vds the region is called resistive, linear or non saturated. Ids is function of vgs and Vds.

When Vds > Vgs - Vt, the channel becomes pinched off. It is called saturation region. The channel no longer reaches drain. Conduction is brought b drift mechanism of electrons under the influence of +ve Vds. Voltage across pinched off channels is Vgs-Vt. Ids is controlled by Vgs and almost independent of drain voltage. Ids depends on

1. Distance between source & Drain.
2. Channel width.
3. Vt.
4. Thickness of Gate insulating layer.
5. Dielectric constant of gate insulator.
6. Mobility of carrier.

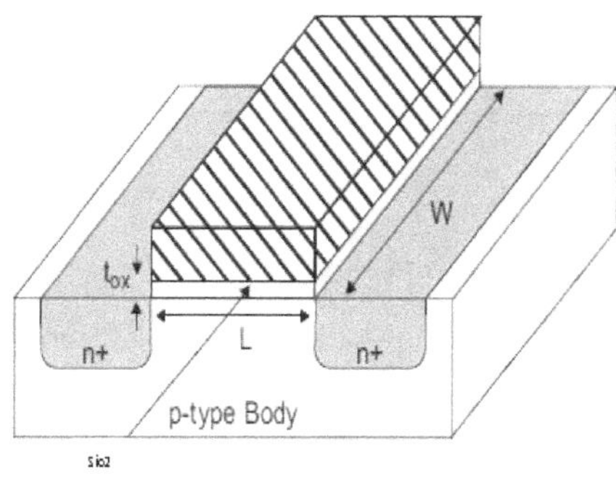

Figure 1.10: Cross Section of NMOS

NMOS Transistor operates in three regions.

1. Cut Off Region

Here the current flow is essentially zero (accumulation mode)

2. Linear Region

It is also called weak inversion region where the drain current is dependent on the gate and the drain voltage w. r. to the substrate.

3. Saturation Region

Channel is strongly inverted and the drain current flow is ideally independent of the drain-source voltage (strong-inversion region).

Operation of NMOS in Accumulation Mode

Accumulation occurs when applied voltage is less than the threshold voltage. The negative charge on the gate attracts holes from the substrate to the oxide-semiconductor interface. Only a small amount of potential is needed to build up the accumulation charge so that almost all of the potential variation is within the oxide.

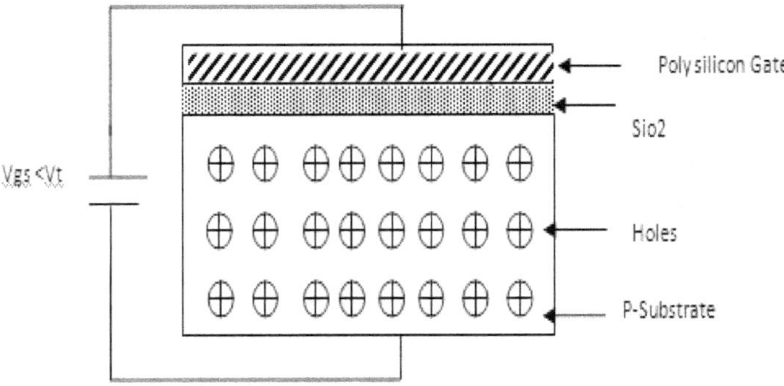

Operation of NMOS in Inversion Mode

As the potential across the semiconductor increases beyond the threshold voltage, another type of negative charge emerges at the oxide-semiconductor interface: this charge is due to minority carriers, which form a so-called inversion layer. As one further increase the gate voltage, the depletion layer width barely increases further since the charge in the inversion layer increases exponentially with the surface potential.

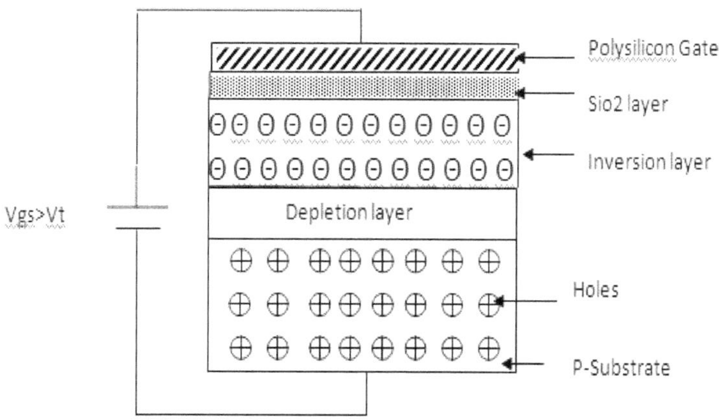

Operation of NMOS in Depletion Mode

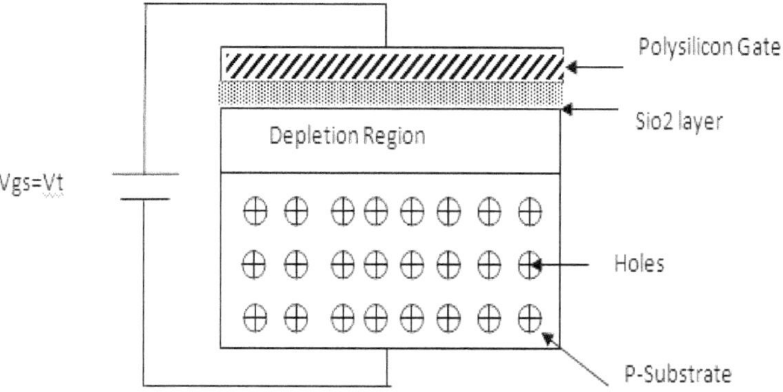

As a more positive voltage than the threshold voltage is applied, a negative charge builds up in the semiconductor. Initially this charge is due to the depletion of the semiconductor starting from the oxide-semiconductor interface.

The depletion layer width further increases with increasing gate voltage. The threshold voltage is voltage required at the gate to generate a conductive channel between source and drain. The conductive channel is generated when the oxide semiconductor is in strong inversion

1.3.   Derivation of Ids in NMOS

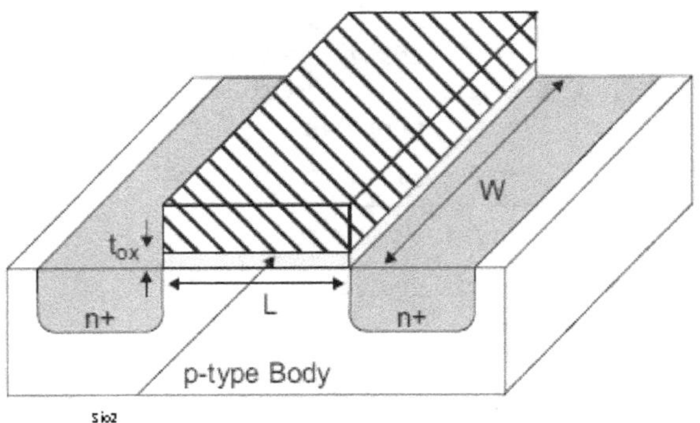

Figure 1.11: NMOS Structure

Q Channel=Cg (Vgc-Vt)

$$\text{Where} \quad Cg = \frac{\varepsilon_{ox} WL}{t_{ox}}$$

$$Vgc = Vgs - \frac{Vds}{2}$$

Velocity $v = \mu E$ where μ= Mobility of charge carrier

E = Vds / L

$$\therefore v = \frac{\mu Vds}{L}$$

$$\text{Ids} = \frac{Q\,Channel}{L/v} = \frac{v\,Q\,Channel}{L} \qquad (1)$$

Substituting the value of v in 1.

$$\text{Ids} \quad = \frac{\mu\,vds}{L}\,\frac{1}{L}\,\frac{\varepsilon_{ox}\,wL}{t_{ox}}\left(vgs - \frac{vds}{2} - vt\right)$$

$$\text{Ids} \quad = \frac{\mu\,\varepsilon_{ox}}{t_{ox}}\,\frac{W}{L}\left[Vgs - V_t - \frac{Vds}{2}\right]vds$$

$$\text{Ids} \quad = \mu.co_x\,\frac{W}{L}\left(Vgs - vt - \frac{vds}{2}\right)vds$$

$$\text{Where} \quad \left[co_x = \frac{\varepsilon_{ox}}{t_{ox}} \right]$$

$$\text{Consider } \beta = \mu.co_x \frac{W}{L} = \mu \frac{\varepsilon_{ox}}{t_{ox}} \frac{W}{L}$$

$$\text{Ids} = \beta \left[Vgs - vt - \frac{vds}{2} \right] vds \qquad (2)$$

In Linear region or resistive region Vgs/2 < < Vgs - vt

Here Ids increases linearly with vds.

Saturation Region

In saturation region Vds >> Vgs - vt

Sub Vds = Vgs – vt in (2)

$$\text{Ids} = \beta \left[vgs - vt - \frac{vds}{2} \right] vds$$

$$= \beta \left[vgs - vt - \frac{vgs - vt}{2} \right] (vgs - vt)$$

$$= \beta \left(\frac{vgs - vt}{2} \right) (vgs - vt)$$

$$= \beta \frac{(vgs - vt)^2}{2} \qquad (3)$$

Cutoff Region

In cutoff vgs > vt and there is no channel. Almost zero current flows from drain to source. The electrons drift from source to drain at a rate proportional to the electric field between the regions.

$$\boxed{\begin{array}{l} \beta = \dfrac{\mu \varepsilon_{ox}}{t_{ox}} \dfrac{W}{L} = \mu cox \dfrac{W}{L} \\[2ex] K \text{ (process gain factor)} = \dfrac{\mu \varepsilon_{ox}}{t_{ox}} \\[2ex] \beta = K \dfrac{W}{L} \\[1ex] \beta = \text{Gain factor (Depends on process parameter \& Geometry)} \end{array}}$$

1.4.   PMOS Transistor Operation

PMOS transistor operation is same as NMOS but the majority charge carrier is holes. The structure of PMOS is shown below.

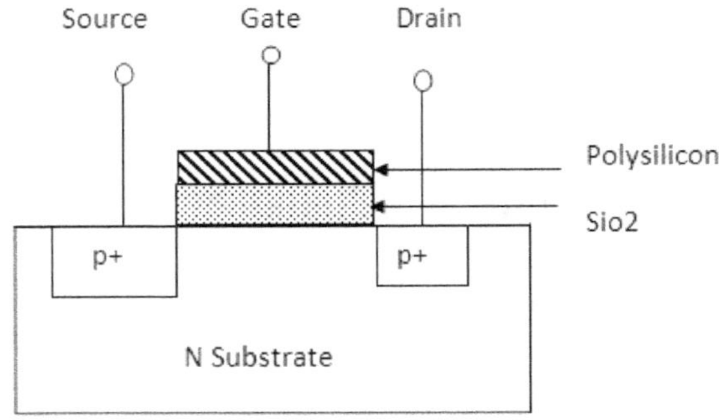

Figure 1.12: PMOS Transistor Structure

1.5.   Fabrication of NMOS

NMOS Fabrication Process

MOS circuits are formed on four basic layers- n diffusion, p diffusion, polysilicon and metal which are isolated from one another by thick or thin silicon dioxide (thinox) insulating layers. Thinox layers include n-diffusion p-diffusion, polysilicon and thinox regions interact so that a transistor is formed where they cross one another. In some processes there may be second metal layers.

- The first step in the n-channel process is to grow an oxide layer on lightly doped p-type substrate (wafer).
- The oxide is etched away (using the diffusion mask) to expose the active regions, such as the sources and drains of all transistors.
- The entire surface is covered with polysilicon.
- The etching process using the polysilicon mask removes all the polysilicon except where it is necessary to define gates. Phosphorus is then diffused into all uncovered silicon, which leads to the formation of source and drain regions.
- Polysilicon (and the oxide underneath it) stops diffusion into any other part of the substrate except in source and drain areas.

- The wafer is then heated, to cover the entire surface with a thin layer of oxide. This layer insulates the bare semiconductor areas from the pathways to be formed on top.
- Oxide is patterned to provide access to the gate, source, and drain regions as required. It should be noted that the task of aligning the polysilicon and diffusion masks is rather easy, because it is only their intersections that define transistor boundaries.
- The formation of a depletion mode transistor requires an additional step of ion implantation. A thin covering of aluminum is deposited over the surface of the oxide.
- Etching then removes all but the requisite wires and contacts.
- Additional metal layers may be laid on top if necessary. It is quite common to use two layers of metal. At places where connections are to be made, areas are enlarged somewhat to assure good inter level contact even when masks are not in perfect alignment.
- In addition to normal contacts, an additional contact is needed in NMOS devices.
- The gate of a depletion mode transistor needs to be connected to its source. This is accomplished by using a buried contact, which is a contact between diffusion and polysilicon.

The final steps involve covering the surface with oxide to provide mechanical and chemical protection for the circuit. This oxide is patterned to form windows which allow access to the aluminum bonding pads.

1.6. Fabrication of PMOS

The PMOS fabrication is same as NMOS fabrication but N type substrate is used instead of P type.

1.7. CMOS Technology

CMOS technology was invented in the mid 1960's. CMOS is an inherently low power circuit technology, with the capability of providing a lower power-delay product comparable in design rules to PMOS and NMOS technologies. Another advantage of CMOS is that there is no direct path between VDD and GND for any combination of inputs. This is the basis for the low static power dissipation in CMOS. Design and Layout of VLSI circuits are greatly influenced by the fabrication process; hence a good understanding of the fabrication cycle helps in designing efficient layouts.

The major drawback of CMOS circuits is that they require more transistors than NMOS circuits. In addition, the CMOS process is more complicated and expensive. On the other hand, power consumption is critical in NMOS and bipolar circuits, while it is less of a concern in CMOS circuits. Driver sizes can be increased in order to reduce net delay in CMOS circuits without any major concern of power. This difference in power consumption makes CMOS technology superior to NMOS and bipolar technologies in VLSI design.

1.7.1. CMOS Inverter

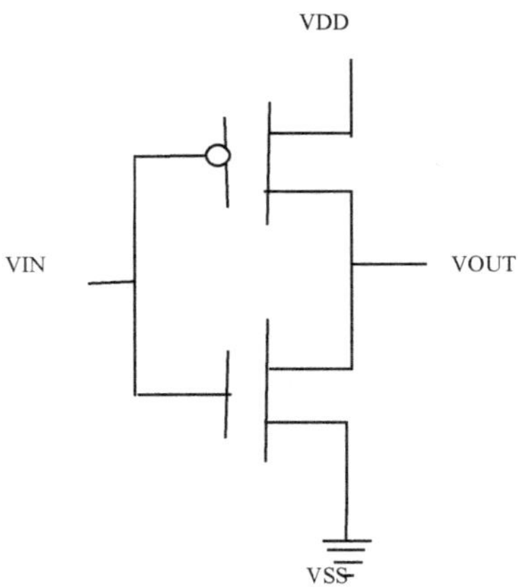

Figure 1.13: CMOS Inverter

A device which is connected to pull the output voltage to the lower supply voltage usually 0V is called pull down device. A device which is connected to pull the output voltage to the upper supply voltage usually VDD is called pull up device. The threshold of both types of devices is slightly negative at low doping densities and differs by 4 times the absolute value of the bulk potential. The threshold of NMOS increases with doping while the threshold of PMOS decreases with doping in the same way. A variation of the threshold voltage due to oxide charge will cause a reduction of both threshold voltages if the charge is positive and an increase if the charge is negative.

Transfer Characteristics of CMOS

CMOS consists of both NMOS and a PMOS. For NMOS, the structure consists of p-type silicon separating two diffused areas of n-type silicon. Similarly, for the PMOS the structure consists of a section on n-type silicon separating two p-type diffused areas. The gate is a control input and it affects the flow of electrical current between the drain and source.

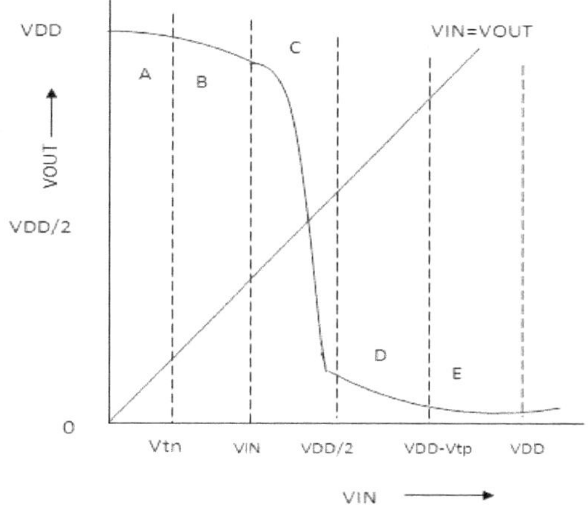

Figure 1.14: Transfer Characteristics of CMOS

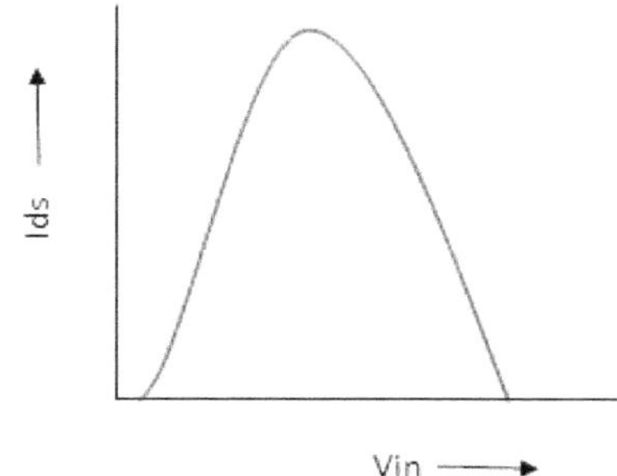

Figure 1.15: Drain Current Flow in CMOS

In region A for which V_{in} = logic 0, the PMOS fully turned on while the NMOS is fully turned off. Thus no current flows through the inverter and the output is directly connected to V_{DD} thorough the p-transistor. In region B the input voltage has increased to a level which just exceeds the threshold voltage of the n-transistor. The NMOS conducts and has a large voltage between source and drain. The PMOS also conducting but with only a small voltage across it, it operates in the unsaid resistive region.

Region D is similar to region B but with the roles of the p-and n-transistors reversed. Current magnitudes in region B and D are small and most of the energy consumed in switching on state to the other is due to the large current which flows in region C. Region C is the region in which the inverter exhibits gain and in which both transistors are in saturation. The currents in each device must be the same since the transistors are in series. So we may write

$$I_{dsp} = - I_{dsn}$$

In region E V_{in} = logic 1, the NMOS is fully on while the p-transistor is fully off. Again no current flows and a good logic 0 appear at the output.

Where,

$$I_{dsp} = \text{ß}_n (V_{in} - V_{DD} - V_{tp})^2 \text{ and}$$

$$I_{dsn} = \text{ß}_n (V_{in} - V_{tn})^2$$

Since both transistors are in saturation, they act as current sources so that the equivalent circuit in this region is two current sources series between V_{DD} and V_{ss} with the output voltage coming from their common point. The region is inherently unstable in consequence and the change over from one logic level to the other is rapid.

V_{tn} = Threshold voltage of n device

V_{tp} = Threshold voltage of P device

Region A

0≤ vin ≤ vtp

In this region N device is off

Idsn = 0

Idsn = -Idsp   ∴ Idsp also equal to zero

Vdsp = Vout - VDD

0 = V out - VDD

Therefore VDD = Vout

Region B

$$V_{tn} \leq V_{in} < \frac{VDD}{2}$$

PMOS act as Linear Resistor and NMOS is in Saturation

$$I_{dsn} = \frac{\beta_n (Vin - Vtn)^2}{2}$$

$$\beta_n = \frac{\mu_n \varepsilon_{ox}}{to_x} \left(\frac{Wn}{Ln} \right)$$

Region C

Here Vin = VDD/2

Both PMOS and NMOS devices are in saturation

PMOS and NMOS devices act as current source.

$$V_{in}\text{-}V_{tn} < V_{out} < V_{tn} \text{-} V_{tp}$$

Since two current sources are in series (unstable) small change in input voltage makes large change in output. This makes output transition very steep.

Region D

$$\frac{VDD}{2} < Vtn \le V_{DD} + V_{tp}$$

PMOS is in saturation and NMOS is in Non saturation

Region E

Here $V_{in} \ge V_{DD}$ - V_{tp}

PMOS is in cutoff (ie Idsp = 0) and NMOS is in linear

$V_{out} = 0$

Region	Condition	p-device	N-device
A	$0 \le$ Vin < Vtn	Non Saturation	Cutoff
B	Vtn $\le$ Vin < VDD/2	Non Saturation	Saturation
C	Vin = VDD/2	Saturation	Saturation
D	VDD/2 < Vin $\le$ VDD- |Vtp|	Saturation	Non Saturation
E	Vin > VDD - |Vtp|	Cutoff	Non Saturation

For CMOS inverter a ratio of $\dfrac{\beta_n}{\beta p} = 1$ may be desirable

If $\beta_n = \beta_p$ if $V_{in} = $ -V_{tp} , then

$$V_{in} = 0.5\ V_{DD}$$

Since only at this point the two factors will be equal. The device geometries must be such that

$$\mu_p\,W_p\,/\,L_p = \mu_n\ W_n\,/\,L_n$$

The hole and electron mobility are inherently unequal and thus it is necessary for the width to length ratio device to be around three times that of the NMOS, namely

$$W/L = 2.5\ W\,/L$$

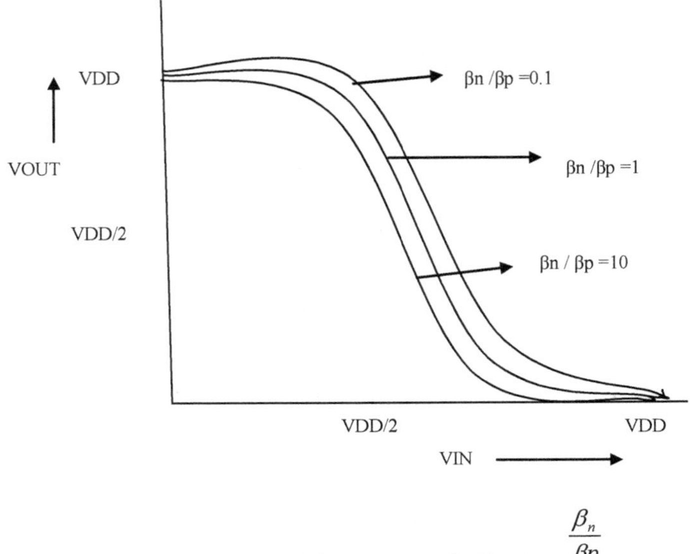

Figure 1.16: Input- Output Characteristics for Varying $\dfrac{\beta_n}{\beta_p}$

1.8. CMOS Fabrication

CMOS has the capability of providing a lower-delay than comparable to NMOS or PMOS technologies. The four dominant CMOS technologies are:

1. P-Well.
2. N-Well.
3. Twin-tub.
4. Silicon on Insulator.

1.8.1. P-Well Process

P-Well processes are preferred in circumstances where the characteristics of NMOS and PMOS are required to be more balanced than that achievable in an N-Well process. Because the transistor that resides in the native substrate tends to have better characteristic, the P-Well process has better PMOS than an N-well process.

A common approach to P-Well CMOS fabrication is to start with moderately doped n-type substrate (wafer), create the p-type well for the NMOS devices, and build the PMOS transitor in the native n-substrate.

The processing steps are:

1. The first mask defines the P-Well. NMOS transistors will be fabricated in this well. Field oxide (FOX) is etched away to allow a deep diffusion.

2. The next mask is called the "thin oxide" or "thinox" mask small of thin oxide are needed to implement transistor gates and allow implantation to for p or n- type diffusions for transistor source /drain regions. The thin oxide area is grown on field oxide areas other terminates for this mask includes active area and island.

3. Polysilicon gate growth involves covering the surface with polysilicon and then etching the required pattern. In this case an invert "Polysilicon" gate regions lead to "self-aligned" source-drain regions.

4. A p-plus (p+) mask is then used to indicate those thin-oxide areas that are to be implanted by p+. Hence a thin-oxide area exposed by the p-plus mask will become a p diffusion area. An n + diffusion in the n-substrate allow an ohmic contact to be made. Following this step, the surface of the chip is covered with a layer of Sio2.

5. Contact cuts are then defined. This involves etching any Sio2 down to the contacted surface, these allow metal to contact diffusion regions of polysilicon regions.

6. Metallization is then applied to the surface and selectively etched.

7. As a final step, the wafer is passivated and openings to the bond pads are etched to allow for wire bonding.

Basically the structure consists of an n-type substrate in which p-devices with suitable masking and diffusion and in order to accommodate n-type devices, a deep P-Well is diffused into the n-type substrate. This diffusion must be carried out with special care since the P-Well doping concentration and depth will affect the threshold voltages as well as the breakdown voltages of the n-transistors. To achieve low threshold voltage (0.6 to 1.0V), deep well diffusion or high resistivity is needed. However, deep well require larger spacing between the NMOS and PMOS transistors and wires because of lateral diffusion resulting in larger chip areas. High resistivity generates latch-up problems In order to achieve narrow threshold tolerances in a typical P-Well process, the well concentration is made higher than the substrate doping density, thereby causing the body effect for n-channel devices to be higher than for PMOS.

1.8.2. N-Well Process

N-Well CMOS circuits are also superior to P-Well because of the lower substrate bias effects on transistor threshold voltage and inherently lower parasitic capacitance associated with source drain regions.

Typically N-Well fabrication steps are similar to a P-Well process, except that an N-Well. The first masking step defines the N-Well regions. This followed by a low phosphorus implant driven in by a high temperature diffusion step to form the N-Wells. The well depth is optimized to ensure against p-substrate to p+ diffusion breakdown without compromising the N-Well to n+ mask separation. The next steps are to define the devices and diffusion paths, grow field oxide deposit and pattern the polysilicon.

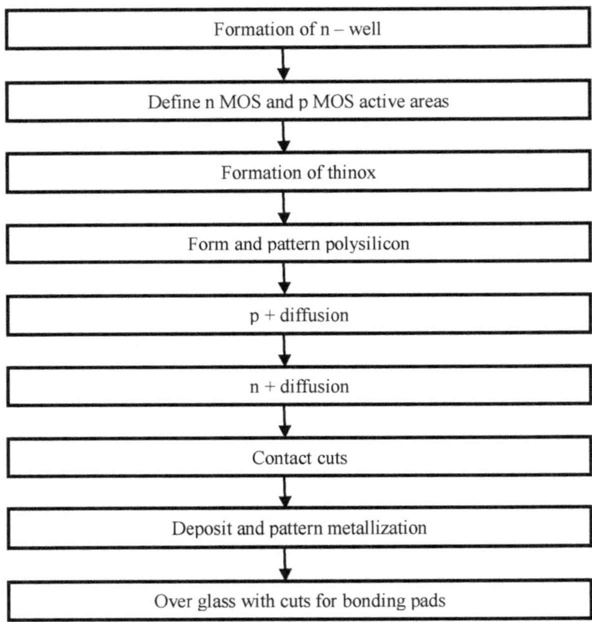

Figure 1.17: Flow Chart for N-Well Process

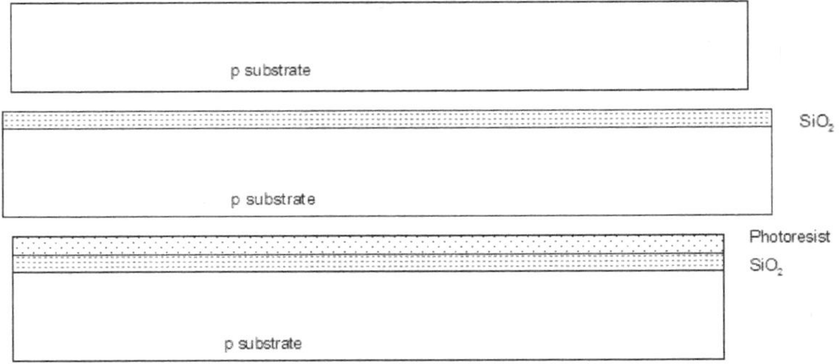

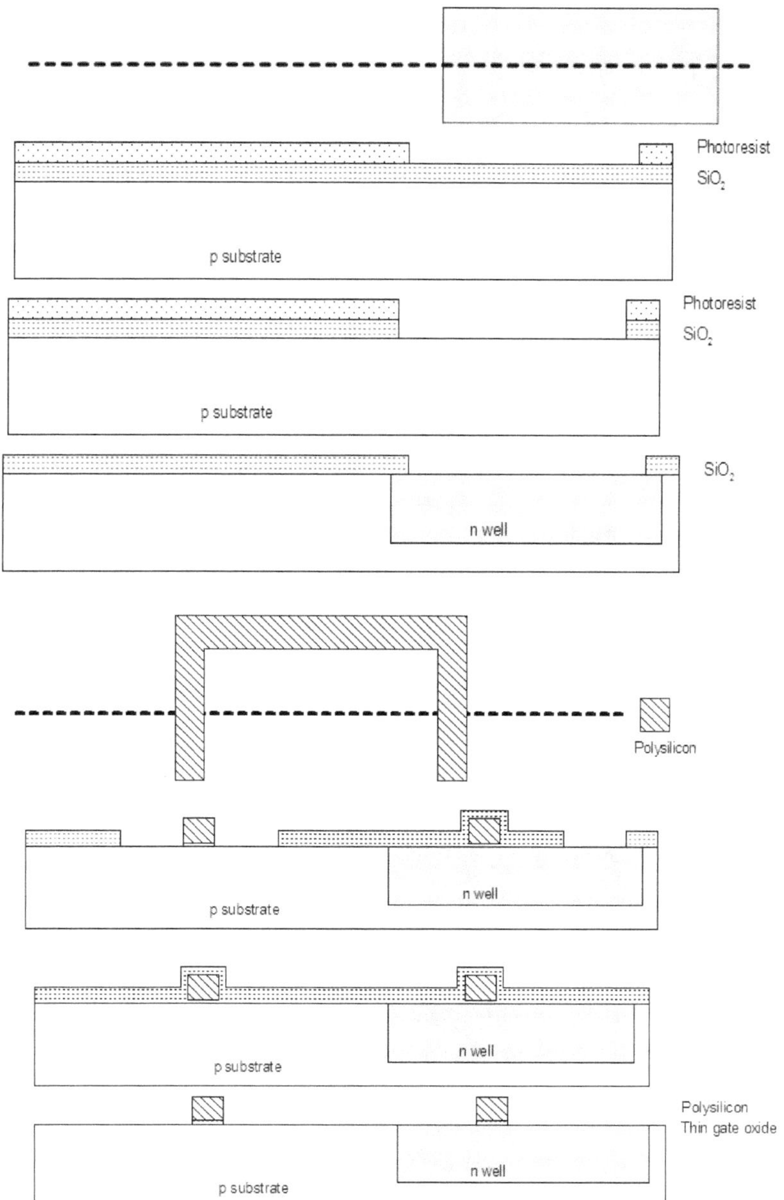

Photoresist
SiO₂
p substrate
Photoresist
SiO₂
p substrate
SiO₂
n well
Polysilicon
n well
p substrate
n well
p substrate
Polysilicon
Thin gate oxide
n well
p substrate

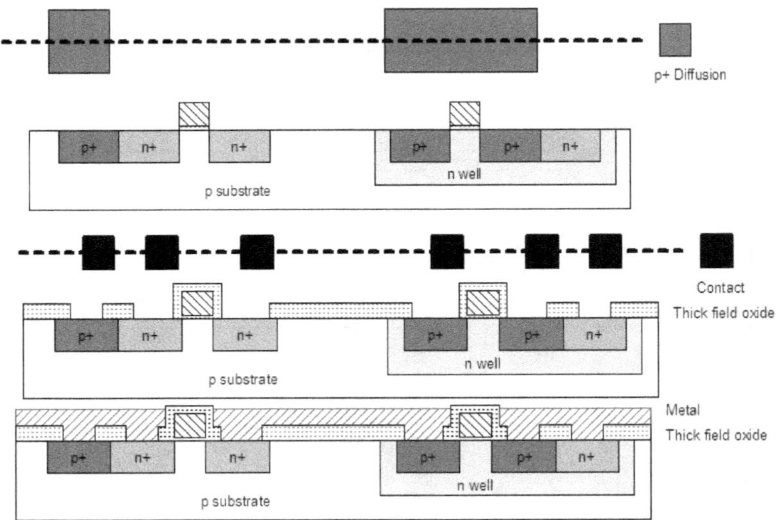

Figure 1.18: N-Well Fabrications

Due to differences in mobility of charge carriers the N-Well process creates non-optimum channel characteristics, such as high junction capacitance and high body effect. The N-Well technology has a distinct advantage of providing optimum device characteristics.

1.8.3. Twin-Tub Process

Twin-tub CMOS technology provides the basis for separate optimization of the p-type and transistors, thus making it possible for threshold voltage, body effect, and the gain associated with NMOS and PMOS to be independently optimized.

Generally the starting material is either n or p substrate with lightly doped epitaxial layer, which is used for protection against latch-up. The aim of epitaxy is to grow high purity silion layers of controlled thickness with accurately determined dopant concentrations distributed homogeneously throughout the layer.

- The starting material is either an n+ or p+ substrate with a lightly doped epitaxial layer, which is used for protection against latch up.
- The process similar to N-Well process entails the following steps.
  - Tub formation.
  - Thin-oxide construction.
  - Source and drain implantations.

- Contact cut definition.
- Metallization.

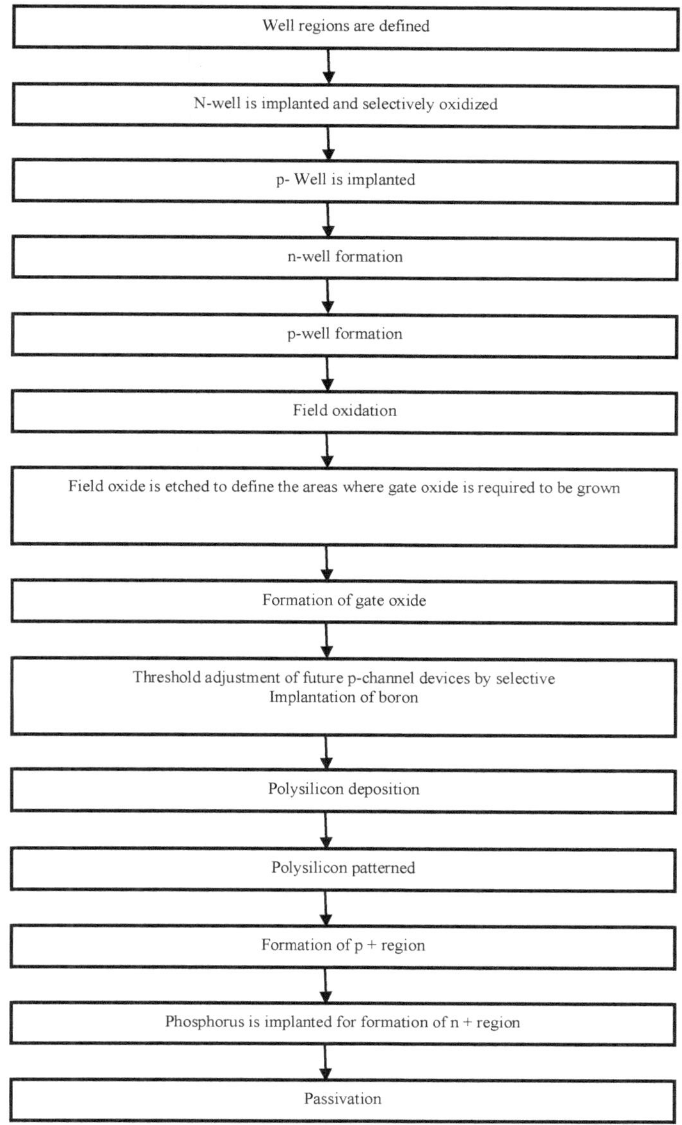

Figure 1.19: Flow Chart for Twin-Tub Fabrication Process

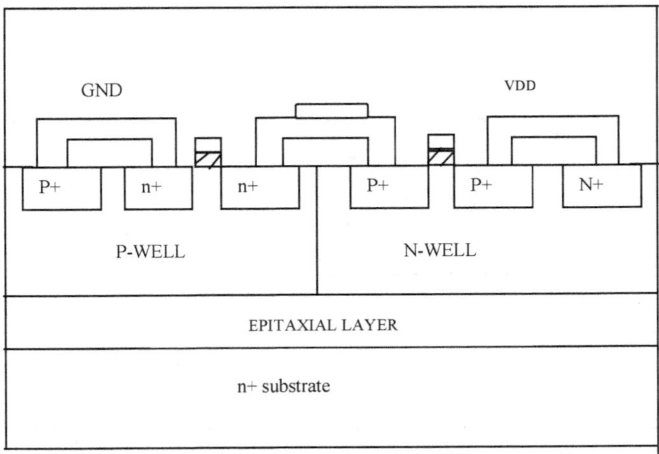

Figure 1.20: Structure of Twin Tub

Since this process provides separate optimized wells, better performance in NMOS, lower capacitance and reduced body effect. It is normally used when compared with a conventional P-Well process.

1.8.4. *Silicon on Insulator Process*

Silicon on insulator (SOI) CMOS processes has several potential advantages such as no latch-up problems, lower parasitic capacitances. In the SOI process a thin layer of crystal silicon film is epitaxial grown on an insulator such as sapphire or magnesium

The steps involves are:

1) A thin film (7-8μm) of very lightly doped n-typed Si is gown over an insulator Sapphire is a commonly used insulator.

2) An isotropic etch is used to etch away the Si except where a diffusion area will be needed.

3) The p-islands are formed next by masking the n-islands with a photoresist. A p-type dopant (boron) is then implanted. It is masked by the photoresist and at the unmasked islands. The p-type islands will become the n-channel devices.

4) The p-islands are then covered with a photoresist and an n-type dopant, phosphorus implanted to form then n-islands .The n-islands will become the p-channel devices.

5) A thin gate oxide (500-600Å) is grown over all of the Si structures .It is normally done by thermal oxidation.

6) A polysilicon film is deposited over the oxide.

7) A polysilicon is then patterned by photo masking and is etched. This defines the polysilicon layer in the structure.

8) The next step is to form the n-doped source and drain of the n-channel devices islands. The n-island is covered with a photoresist and an n-type dopant (phosphorus) implant.

9) A layer of phosphorus glass is deposited over the entire structure. The glass is etched for contact cut locations. The metallization layer is formed. A final passivation layer over phosphorus glass is deposited and etched over bonding pad locations.

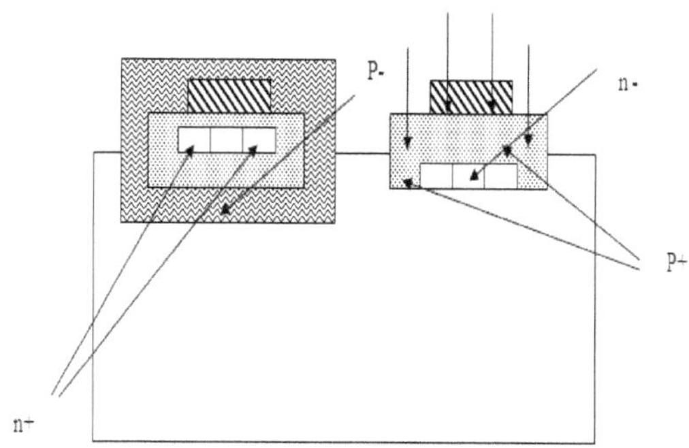

Figure 1.21: Structure of SOI

The advantages of SOI technology are:

Due to the absence of wells, denser structures than bulk silicon can be obtained. Low capacitances provide the basis of very fast circuits. No field-inversion problems exist. No latch-up due to isolation of NMOS and PMOS by insulating substrate. As there is no conducting substrate, there are no body effect problems.

Disadvantages of SOI

- Lack of substrate diodes makes I/O protection difficult.
- Coupling capacitance still exists.
- More expensive to build.

1.9. Latch Up Problem

Latch-up is a condition in which the parasitic components give rise to the establishment of low resistance conducting paths between VDD and VSS with disastrous results. Careful control during fabrication is necessary to avoid this problem.

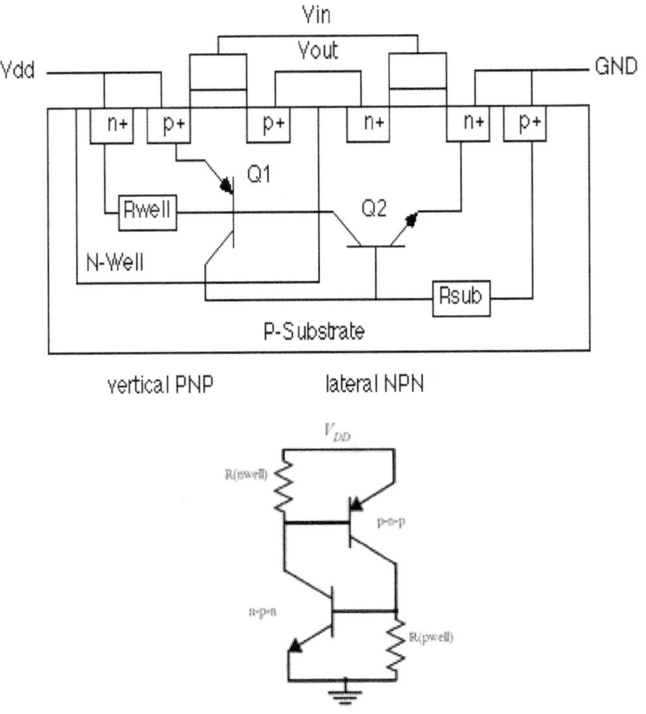

Figure 1.22: Latch Up Problem

1.10. Non- Ideal I-V Effects

The I-V characteristics designed so far neglect many effects that are important in MOS deep-submicron processes.

Some of these effects include:

- Velocity Saturation and Mobility Degradation.
- Channel length modulation.
- Sub threshold conduction.
- Tunneling.
- Junction leakage.
- Body effect.
- Temperature and Geometry dependence.

1.10.1. Threshold Voltage- Body Effect

The voltage applied to the back contact affects the threshold voltage of a MOSFET. The voltage difference between the source and the bulk changes the width of the depletion layer and therefore also the voltage across the oxide due to the change of the charge in the depletion region. This results in a modified expression for the threshold voltage. Vt is not constant with respect to the voltage difference between the substrate and source of MOS. This is known as substrate- bias effect or body effect.

$$Vt = Vt + Y\left[\sqrt{2\phi s + |vsb|} - \sqrt{2\phi s}\right]$$

ϕs = surface potential at threshold

Vsb = substrate bias

Vto = Threshold voltage for Vsb = o

r = constant that describes substrate bias effect.

$$Y = \frac{1}{co_x} \sqrt{2q\,\varepsilon_{si}\,NA}$$

q = charge on electron

ε_{ox} = Dielectric constant of Si O2

εSi = Dielectric constant of Silicon substrate

$$\phi_s = 2\,v_T\,\ln\frac{N_A}{ni}$$

In SPICE Model

Y = GAMMA in SPICE Model.

N_A = N_{SUB}

Vt0 = VT0

The cut off region is defined as sub threshold region. Ids is very small nearly zero in this region.

1.10.2. Channel Length Modulation

MOS device assumes carrier mobility as constant ie It does not take into account the variation in channel length due to charges in Vds.

For long channel length, there is no need to consider this parameter. As devices are scaled down the channel length variation should be taken into account.

When MOS device is in saturation, channel effective length decreases.

$$\text{Leff} = L - \text{Lshort}$$

As L decreases $\left(\dfrac{W}{L}\right)$ increases thereby increasing β

$$I_{ds} = \frac{kW}{2L}\left(vgs - vt\right)^2 \left(1 + \lambda vds\right)$$

K = process Gain factor = $\dfrac{\mu\varepsilon_{ox}}{t_{ox}}$

λ = Channel modulation factor

Mobility variation (Mobility degradation)

$$\mu = \frac{\underline{\text{Average carrier draft velocity (v)}}}{\text{Electric field (E)}}$$

Electrons have higher mobility than electrons.

Mobility decreases with increase in doping concentration and Temperature

1.10.3. Fowler - Nordheim Tunneling

Due to this effect Sio_2 thickness is decreased. So current can flow through gate to source or drain. This effect limits the scaling of SiO_2 thickness.

1.10.4. Drain Punch Through

When drain is at high enough voltage with respect to source, the depletion region around the drain may extend to the source, thus causing current to flow irrespective of gate voltage. This is known as punch through. Currently, this effect is used in I/O protection circuits to limit the voltages across internal circuit nodes, although it will impact design as devices are scaled down by requiring that internal circuit voltages be reduced to a point where the effect does not occur.

1.10.5. Impact Ionization

As length of the gate in MOS transistor is reduced, electric field at drain of transistor increases. For submicron gate lengths, the electrons imparted with high energy to become hot. These hot electrons dislodged holes movement forms the substrate current.

1.11. CMOS Process Enhancements

Transistors with Multiple threshold voltages are used. Low threshold devices are faster and offer higher leakage. High threshold devices are just opposite to Low threshold devices.

- **Silicon on Insulator**

  As the name suggests transistors are fabricated on an insulator (SiO_2 or sapphire), insulating substrate eliminates capacitance between the source/drain and body. It increases speed and decreases leakage currents.

- **High-k gate dielectrics**

  Transistors need high gate capacitance to attract charges to the channel . Thicker gates that leak less can be made with high-k materials.

- **Low leakage transistors**

  Scaling transistors causes exponential increase in sub threshold leakages.This can be improved using gate structure where gate is placed on more than one silicon of the channel

- **Higher mobility**

  It is achieved by Si-Ge for bipolar transistors in the same conventional CMOS process. MOS transistors fabricated with organic chemicals used only for very specific applications as devices are very inexpensive to manufacture.

- **High-voltage transistors**

  High voltage MOSEETs can be integrated into conventional CMOS processes.

- **Low-k Dielectrics**

  Low-k dielectrics between wires are attractive as they decrease wire capacitance, reduces wire delay and power consumption.

1.12. Circuit Elements

- **Capacitors**

  In conventional CMOS, capacitors can be created using the gate and source/drain, a diffusion area (to ground or Vss) or a parallel metal plate capacitor.

- **Resistors**

  In conventional CMOS, resistors can be built from any layer, where the final resistance depends on the resistivity (resistance per unit area) of the layer. Large resistance in small areas is built using polysilicon or diffusion Another enhancement that requires additional processing steps is to allow nichrome that produces high quality resistors.

1.13. Electrical Properties of CMOS

It discusses the Resistance and capacitance effects.

1.13.1. Resistance

Resistance can be expressed as

$$R = \frac{\ell}{E}\frac{L}{W} \qquad Rs = \frac{\ell}{t} = \text{sheet Resistance}$$

When Vgs > Vt, MOSFET always introduce parasitic resistance and capacitance that effects circuit operation.

$$r_n = \frac{\partial vds}{\partial Ids}$$

Ids is inversely proportional to βn

$$R_n \ \alpha \ \frac{1}{\beta_n} = \frac{1}{kn\left(\dfrac{Wn}{Ln}\right)}$$

At Vdd, $\qquad$ vs = Vgs - vt$_n$ and Vgs = VDD

$$R_n = \frac{Vgs - Vt_n}{Ids} = \frac{Vgs - Vt_n}{Ids}$$

We know Ids $= \dfrac{\beta_n}{2}(Vgs - vt_n)^2 \, inSatuaration$

$$R_n = \frac{Vgs - Vt_n}{\dfrac{\beta n}{2}(Vgs - Vtn)^2}$$

$$R_n = \frac{2}{\beta_n \, (Vgs - vtn)} = \frac{2}{\beta n(V_{DD} - Vt_n)}$$

For VDS = VDD

$$R_n = \frac{VDD}{Ids} = \frac{VDD}{\dfrac{\beta n}{2}(vgs - vtn)^2}$$

$$R_n = \frac{2\,VDD}{\beta_n(Vgs - vtn)^2} \qquad\qquad (1)$$

When Vgs = VDD

$$R_n = \frac{2\,VDD}{\beta n\,(VDD - vtn)^2} \qquad (2)$$

Similarly for PMOS

$$R_n = \frac{2}{\beta p\,(VDD - |vtp|)} \qquad (3)$$

$$R_n = \frac{2\,VDD}{\beta p\,(VDD - |vtp|)^2} \qquad (4)$$

1.13.2. Capacitance

Two parallel plates separated by thin dielectric oxide forms capacitance.

$$Cg = Cox\ W\ L$$

In addition to gate, the source and drain also have capacitance. The capacitances which are not fundamental to the operation as the device but affect performance are called parasitic capacitance. Csb and Cdb arise due to reverse biased PN diode between source & drain diffusion and body. It is called diffusion capacitance.

$$\iota = C\,\frac{dv}{dt}, \quad \iota = C\,\frac{\Delta v}{\Delta t}$$

Capacitances tend to slow down the switching speed of circuits .The capacitance related to MOS (Gate capacitances) are denoted by Cgs, Cgd and Cgb.

The Capacitances due to PN junctions (diffusion capacitance) are denoted by Csb, Cdb. Gate Capacitance is necessary to attract charge to invert the channel. So high gate capacitance is required to get high Ids.

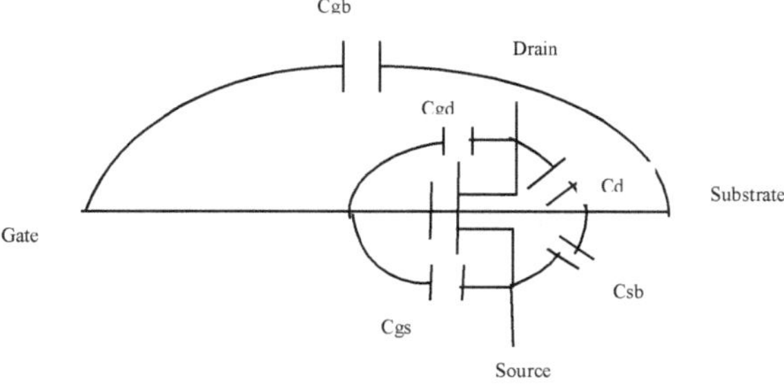

Figure 1.23: MOS Capacitance Model

Table 1.1: MOS Gate Capacitance

Parameter	Cutoff	Linear	Saturation
Cgb	Co	0	0
Cgs	0	Co/2	2/3 Co
Cgd	0	Co/2	0
Cg= Cgs+ Cgd+ Cgb	Co	Co	2/3 Co

Considering Co = Co_x WL

Diffusion Capacitance

Diffusion capacitance depends on both the area As and side wall parameter Ps of the source diffusion region.

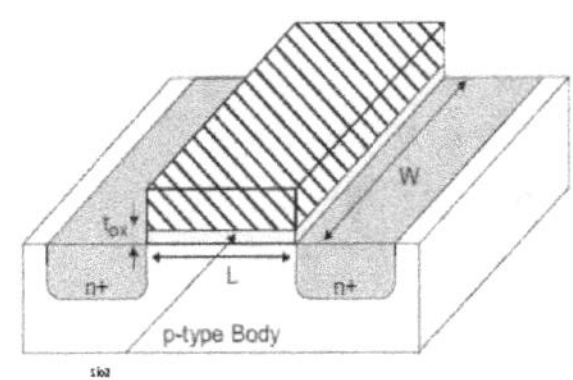

Figure 1.24: Geometry of Diffusion

$$As = W * D$$

$$\text{Perimeter } P_S = 2 * W + 2 * D$$

Total source parasitic capacitance Csb = A_S.Cjbs + Ps. CjbSSw

$$Cjbs = CJ \left(1 + \frac{Vsb}{\psi_o}\right)^{-MJ}$$

CJ = Junction capacitance

MJ = Junction grading coefficient in the range of 0.5 to 0.33

$$\psi_o = V_T \ln \frac{N_A N_D}{r^{,2}}$$

(Build in potential) $\quad V_T = \dfrac{KT}{q}$

K= Boltzmann's constant

$$Cjbssw = CJSW \left(1 + \frac{Vsb}{\psi_o}\right)^{-MJSW}$$

Total diffusion capacitance between source and body is

$$Csb = A_S. C_J \left(1 + \frac{Vsb}{\psi_o}\right)^{-MJ} + PS. C_{JSW} \left(1 + \frac{Vsb}{\psi_o}\right)^{-MJSW}$$

1.14. Scaling

Scaling of MOS transistor is concerned with systematic reduction of overall dimensions of the devices as allowed by the available technology, while preserving the geometric ratios found in the larger devices.

Scaling device is obtained by applying dimensionless factor to

- All dimensions including those vertical to surface.
- Device voltages.
- Concentration densities.

Constant Field Scaling

In constant Field scaling Channel length L, W, t_{ox}, density N, depletion layer thickness, Vt and Ids are scaled by constant parameter. Constant Field scaling increases the electric field in devices. Static power dissipation Pst & Pdyn decreases by $\dfrac{1}{S^2}$ .In Industry standards S = $\sqrt{2}$

The substrate doping N_A is increased by S. Because both distance and voltage are scaled equally; the electric field remains constant.

Table 1.2: Constant Field Scaling

Parameter	Constant Field scaling
Length L	1/s
Width W	1/s
t_{ox} - Gate oxide thickness	1/s
VDD - Supply voltage	1/s
Vt - Threshold voltage	1/s
N_A - substrate doping	s
Device Characteristics	
$\beta = \dfrac{1}{t_{ox}}\dfrac{W}{L}$	s
Ids	1/s
$R = \dfrac{VDD}{Ids}$	1
Gate capacitance $C = \dfrac{WL}{t_{ox}}$	1/s
Gate delay λ = RC	1/s
$f = \dfrac{1}{\xi}$	s
Dynamic power dissipation	$1/s^2$

Following are the key principles for low power design.

1. Use lowest possible supply voltage
2. Use smallest Geometry, highest frequency devices but operating them at lowest possible frequency.
3. Use parallelism & pipelining.
4. Power management by disconnecting the power source when in idle.

1.15. Layout Design

Chip layout can be characterized as the step in the design hierarchy where an electronic circuit is transferred to a silicon description. The layout designer is responsible for creating the patterns on every layer. Layout is performed on a computer using layout editor. Metal to Metal contact is called via. Diffusion or poly to metal is called as contact.

1.15.1. Layout Rules

It is a prescription for preparing the photo masks used in the fabrication of IC. CMOS Processes tend to be identified by the smaller feature size that can be fabricated reliably on a chip. Layout design is used to create the chip layer pattern. The efficient layout design utilizes minimum width and minimum spacing. The minimum width and spacing   values are specified for every layer on the chip. They are part of larger group of geometrical specifications that are collectively known as layout design rules. Design rule checker is provided in the layout editor to find Design rule violations. The rules are defined in terms of feature size (widths), separations and overlap. Types of Layout rules are

1. Micron rule (μm).
2. Lambda based rule (λ).

MOSIS Scalable CMOS Rules (SCMOS RULES) are expressed in terms of λ. It allows some degree of scaling. It is available with λ = 1.0 μm, λ = 0.80 μm & λ=0.35μm. Rules called (i) Well rule (ii) Transistor rule(discuss about NMOS & PMOS inside CMOS) (iii) Contact rules (iv) Metal rules (v) via rules are framed. Logic gates use minimum length devices for least delay, area and power consumption.

Design rules mainly address two issues.

- The geometrical reproduction of features that can be reproduced by the mask making and lithographical process.
- The interactions between different layers.

Table 1.3: SCMOS Rules

No.	Description	In Terms of λ
A.	**N-Well layer**	
	Minimum size	10λ
	Minimum spacing (wells at same potential)	6λ
	Minimum spacing (wells at different potential)	8λ
B.	**Active Area**	
	Minimum size	3λ
	Minimum spacing	3λ
	N well overlap of p+	5λ
	N well space to n+	5λ
	N well space to p+	3λ
C.	**Poly**	
	Minimum size	2λ
	Minimum spacing	2λ
	Spacing to Active	1λ
	Gate Extension	2λ
D.	**p+, n+ for short**	
	Minimum overlap of Active	2λ
	Minimum size	7λ
E.	Contact	
	Minimum size	2λ
	Minimum spacing (poly)	2λ
F.	**Metal 1**	
	Minimum size	3λ
	Minimum spacing	3λ
G	**Via**	
	Minimum size	2λ
	Minimum spacing Via	3λ
	Exact Size	2λ x 2λ
	Via to Via Spacing	.3λ
	METAL 1 Overlap of Via	1λ
	Via Spacing	
	Via To Polysilicon	2λ
	Via (On Polysilicon) to Polysilicon.	2λ
	Via To Active	2λ
H	**METAL 2**	
	Minimum Width.	3λ
	Minimum Spacing	4.λ
	Overlap of Via	3λ

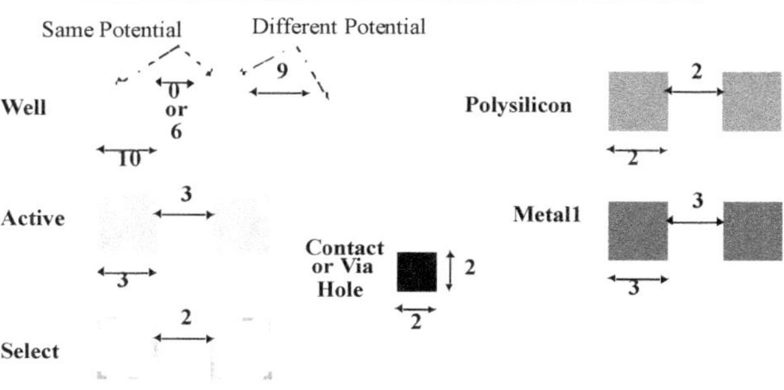

Figure 1.25: Design Rule

1.16. Stick Diagram

It is used to convey layer information through the use of colour code.

Table 1.4: Colour Representation of Layers

Colour Representation	Layers
	NMOS
	PMOS
	METAL
	POLYSILICON
	P DIFFUSION
	CONTACT
	N DIFFUSION

In CMOS a demarcation line is drawn to avoid touching of p-diff with n-diff. All PMOS must lie on one side of the line and all NMOS will have to be on the other side.

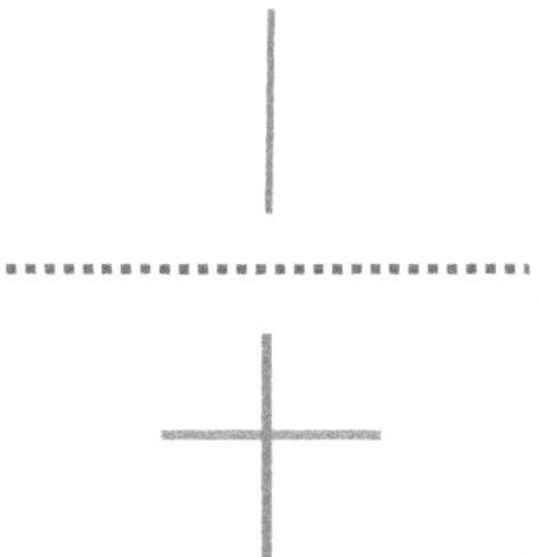

Figure 1.26: Demarcation Line in CMOS

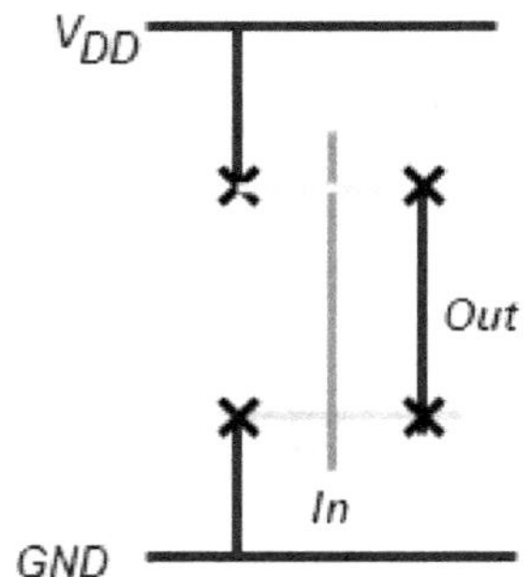

Figure 1.27: Stick Diagram of Inverter

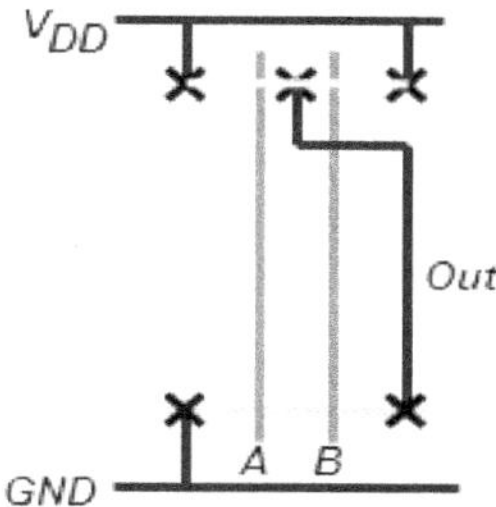

Figure 1.28: Stick Diagram of NAND Gate

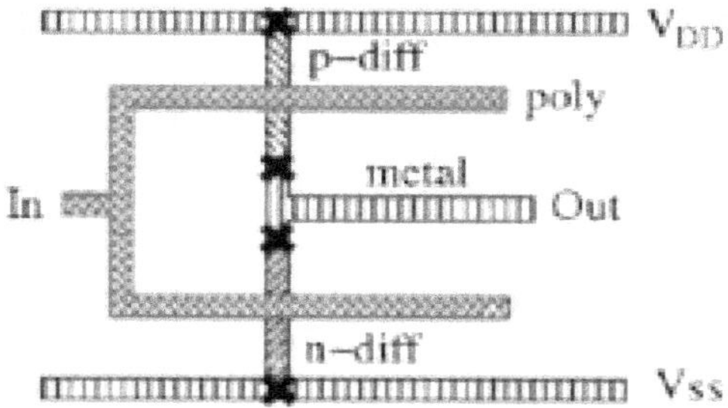

Figure 1.29: Layout of Inverter

1.17. MOSFET Modeling with SPICE

SPICE (A simulation program with Integrated circuit emphasis) was developed in 1970s at Berkeley. It solves the nonlinear differential equations describing components such as transistors resistors, capacitors and voltage sources. HSPICE is widely used in Industry.

Table 1.5: Representation of Components

Letter	Element
R	Resistor
C	Capacitor
L	Inductor
K	Mutual Inductor
V	Voltage source
I	Current source
M	MOSFET
D	Diode
Q	BJT
W	Lossy transmission line

Table 1.6: Representation of Units

Letter	Unit
a	atto 10^{-18}
f	femto 10^{-15}
p	pico 10^{-12}
n	nano 10^{-9}
u	micro 10^{-6}
m	milli 10^{-3}
k	kilo 10^{3}
x	mega 10^{6}
g	giga 10^{9}

Voltage Source Representation

DC Voltage source Vdd that sets voltage to 2.5v is expressed as

Vdd vdd gnd 2.5

Pulse sources are defined as

Rise time	=	100 PS
Fall time	=	100 PS
Delay time	=	0 PS
PW	=	300 PS
per (Time period)	=	800 PS

PULSE	v_1	v_2	td	tr	tf	pw	per
PULSE	0	1.8	0PS	100 PS	100PS	300PS	800PS

Passive Components

Resistor (Connected between input and output) is given as

R1   in   out   2k

Capacitor (Connected between output and ground) is given as

C1   out   gnd   100f

Finding the voltage, current etc by applying DC voltage is called DC response. Finding the response by applying frequency varying signals of pulse, Saw tooth and Triangular etc is called transient response.

NMOS Transistor

Mname drain gate some body type W = < >   L = < >

M   d   g   gnd   gnd   NMOS W = 0.36 u   L = .18 u

PMOS

M d g   vdd   vdd   PMOS - W = 0.36u L = 0.18 u.

. dc   represents   dc analysis

. tran represents   Transient analysis

Sample Netlist is Given Below

Vgs g gnd   0

Vds d gnd   0

M$_1$ d g gnd gnd NMOS W = 0.36 u L = 0.18 u

. dc vds 0 1.8 0.05 SWEEP Vgs 0 1.8   0.3

. end

. dc command varies the voltage source vdd from 0 to 1.8v in increments of 0.05v.

This is repeated multiple times as vgs swept from 0 to 1.8 v in increments of 0.3v

1.17.1. Device Models

SPICE provides a wide variety of MOS transistor models with various tradeoffs between complexity and accuracy. Level 1 & Level 3 are not accurate models. BSIM models are more accurate and presently most widely used.

Level 1

Level 1 model is closely related to Shockley model enhanced with channel length modulation and body effect.

$$Ids = \begin{cases} 0 & vgs\,c\,vt & cut\,off \\ KP\dfrac{Weff}{Leff}\,(1+LAMBDA\,vds) & \left(Vgs-vt-\dfrac{Vds}{2}\right)vds & vds<vgs-vt\ Linea \\ \dfrac{KP}{2}\dfrac{Weff}{Leff}\,(1+LAMBDA\,vds) & (vgs-vt)^2 & vds>vgs-vt\ satu \end{cases}$$

K is denoted here as   KP. It is a Model parameter.

$$Vt = VTO+GAMMA\left(\sqrt{PHI+Vsb}-\sqrt{PHI}\right)$$

v_{to} = zero bias threshold voltage

r = Body effort coefficient

ϕs = surface potential

Level 2 and 3 Model

It adds efforts of velocity saturation, mobility degradation and sub threshold conduction. It provides similar accuracy and faster simulation times. However these models do not provide good fit for measurement of IV characteristics of modern transistor.

BSIM Model (Berkeley Short Channel IGFET Model)

It uses enormous number of parameters to fit to the behavior of modern transistors. Different versions BSIM are available.

Features of this model include.

- Continuous and differentiable I-V characteristics across sub threshold, linear and saturation regions for good convergence.
- Detailed threshold voltage model including body effect.
- Velocity saturation, mobility degradation and other short channel effects.
- Multiple gate capacitance model
- Diffusion capacitance & resistance model.

1.17.2. *Diffusion Capacitance Model*

The PN Junction between source or drain and the body forms a reverse biased diode. Diffusion capacitance determines delay of the gate independent on area and perimeter.

SPICE models contain parameters CJ, CJSW, PB, PHP, MJ and MJSW.

The diffusion capacitance between source and is body is computed by

$$Cjb = As.CJ. \left(1 + \frac{Vsb}{PB}\right)^{-MJ} + Ps\ CJSW. \left(1 + \frac{Vsb}{PHP}\right)^{-MJSW}$$

For analyzing the drain equation S is replaced by D.

BSIM3 models take into account the different sidewall capacitances on the edge adjacent to the gate.

$$Csb = AS.CJ \left(1 + \frac{Vsb}{PB}\right)^{-MJ} + (PS - W).\ CJSW \left(1 + \frac{Vsb}{PBSW}\right)^{-MJSW}$$

$$+ W.\ CJSWG \left(1 + \frac{Vsb}{PBSWG}\right)^{-MJSWG}$$

For simulation ACM (Area Calculation method) is used by SPICE to control geometry.

For ACM = 0, user has to specify area & perimeter.

A = 1, 2,3 .... Takes non zero default value when area & perimeter are not specified.

PB = Ψo (Built in potential) for Area.

PHP = Ψo for perimeter.

Vsb = voltage difference between source & bulk.

1.18. Propagation Delay

tpHL: Propagation delay from Input to rising output crossing VDD/2

tpLH: Propagation delay from Input to falling output crossing VDD/2

Average propagation delay is given as

$$\text{tpd: (tpHL + tpLH)}/2$$
$$V_{50\%} = 1/2 \ (VOL+VOH)$$

Rise time: Time for a waveform to rise from 10% to 90% of its steady state value.

Fall time: Time for a waveform to fall from 90% to 10% of its steady state value.

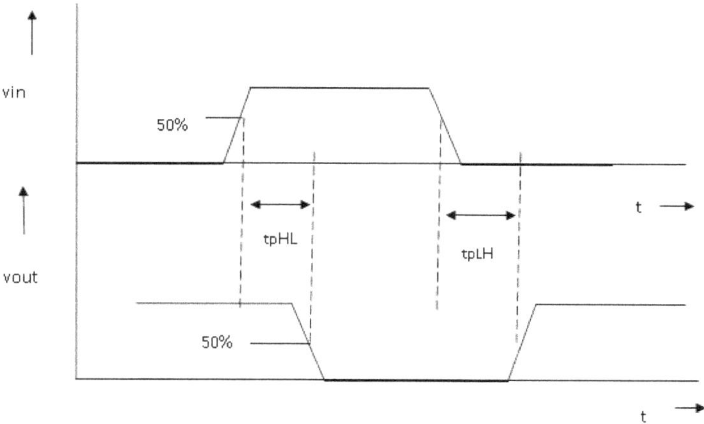

Figure 1.30: Propagation Delay

1.19. Noise Margin

Noise margin is the amount of noise that a CMOS could withstand without compromising the operation of the circuit. Noise margin does make sure that any signal which is "Logic1" with finite noise added to it is still recognized as "Logic1" and not "Logic0".It is the difference between signal and noise value.

NM_l (Noise margin low) = Vil- Vol

NM_h (Noise Margin high) = Voh- Vih

Where Vih is slightly less than V_{DD} and Vil is slightly higher than V_{SS} for practical circuits.

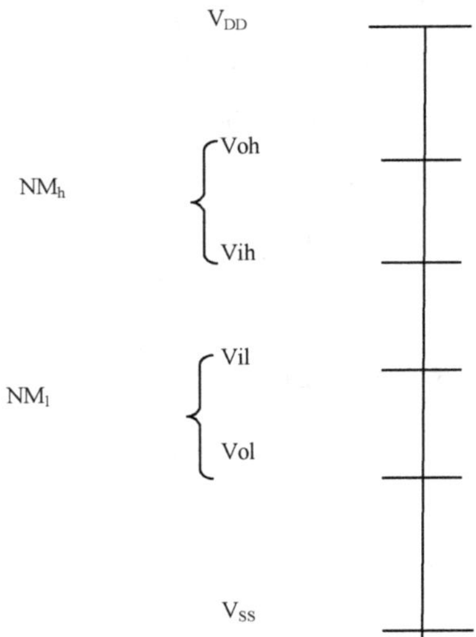

Figure 1.31: Noise Margin Representations

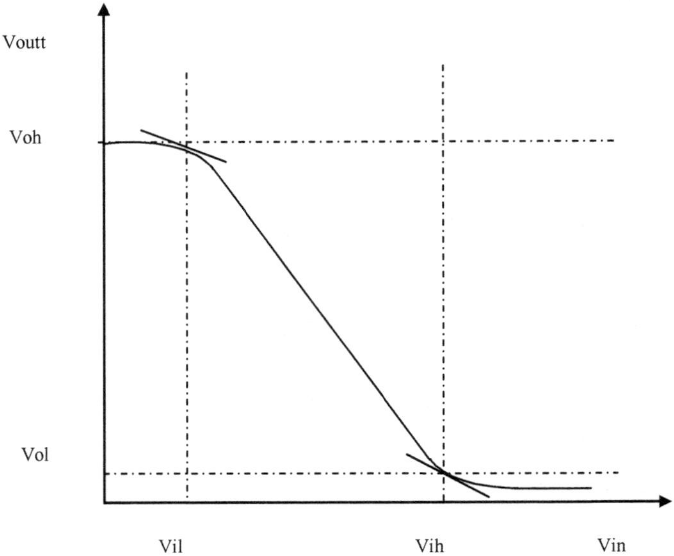

Figure 1.32: Graph of Noise Margin Calculation

2 Marks with Answer

1. What is Intrinsic and Extrinsic Semiconductor?

   The pure Silicon is known as Intrinsic Semiconductor.

   When impurity is added with pure Silicon, its electrical properties are varied.

   This is known as Extrinsic Semiconductor.

2. What is CMOS Technology?

   The fabrication of an IC using CMOS transistors is known as CMOS Technology.

   CMOS transistor is nothing but an inverter made up of an NMOS and PMOS transistor connected in series.

3. Give the advantages of CMOS IC?
   1. Size is less.
   2. High Speed.
   3. Less Power Dissipation.

4. What are four generations of Integration Circuits?
   1. SSI (Small Scale Integration).
   2. MSI (Medium Scale Integration).
   3. LSI (Large Scale Integration).
   4. VLSI (Very Large Scale Integration)

5. Give the variety of Integrated Circuits?
   1. More Specialized Circuits.
   2. Application Specific Integrated Circuits (ASICs).
   3. Systems-On-Chips.

6. Give the advantages of IC?
   1. Size is less.
   2. High Speed.
   3. Less Power Dissipation.

7. Give the variety of Integrated Circuits?.
   1. More Specialized Circuits.
   2. Application Specific Integrated Circuits (ASICs).
   3. Systems-On-Chips.

8. Why NMOS technology is preferred more than PMOS technology?

   N-channel transistors have greater switching speed when compared to PMOS transistors. Hence, NMOS is preferred than PMOS.

9. What are the different MOS layers?

    1. n-diffusion.

    2. p-diffusion.

    3. Polysilicon.

    4. Metal.

10. What are the different layers in MOS transistor?

    The layers are Substrate, diffused Drain & Source, Insulator (SiO2) & Gate.

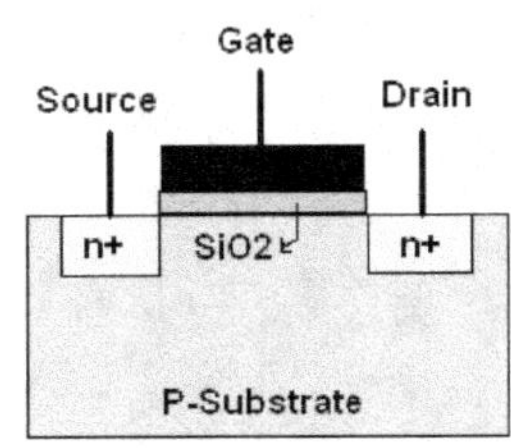

11. What are the different operating regions for an MOS transistor?

    1. Cutoff Region.

    2. Non- Saturated (Linear) Region.

    3. Saturated Region.

12. What is Enhancement mode transistor?

    The device that is normally cut-off with zero gate bias is called Enhancement mode transistor.

13. What is Depletion mode device?

    The Device that conducts with zero gate bias is called Depletion mode device.

14. When the channel is said to be pinched off?

    If a large Vds is applied, this voltage will deplete the inversion layer. This Voltage effectively pinches off the channel near the drain.

15. What are the steps involved in manufacturing of IC?

    1. Silicon wafer Preparation.

    2. Epitaxial Growth.

    3. Oxidation.

    4. Photo-lithography.

    5. Diffusion.

    6. Ion Implantation.

7. Isolation technique.

8. Metallization.

9. Assembly processing & Packaging.

16. What is meant by Epitaxy?

Epitaxy means arranging atoms in single crystal fashion upon a single crystal substrate.

17. What are the processes involved in photo lithography?

1. Masking process.

2. Photo etching process.

These are important processes involved in photolithography.

18. What is the purpose of masking in fabrication of IC?

Masking is used to identify the location in which Ion-Implantation should not take place.

19. What lire the materials used for masking?

Photo resist, Si02, SiN, Poly Silicon.

20. What are the types of Photo etching?

Wet etching and dry etching are the types of photo etching.

21. What is diffusion process? What are doping impurities?

Diffusion is a process in which impurities are diffused into the Silicon chip at 1000°C temperature.

22. What is Ion-Implantation process?

It is process in which the Si material is doped with an impurity by making the accelerated impurity atoms to strike the Si layer at high temperature.

23. What are the various Silicon wafer Preparation?

1. Crystal growth & doping.

2. Ingot trimming & grinding.

3. Ingot slicing.

4. Wafer polishing & etching.

5. Wafer cleaning.

24. What are the different types of oxidation?

The two types of oxidation are Dry & Wet Oxidation.

It is a process in which a substance adds on oxygen or loses hydrogen. The current definition of oxidation is the process in which a substance loses electrons.

25. What is etching process?

The etching process involves sheets of metal, usually made of copper or zinc, and acid used to etch the print onto the metal. The artist can use complicated methods to create different effects, but always relies on acid to etch the plate.

26. What are the various etching process used in SOI process?

Various etching process used in SOI are:

- Isotropic etching process.
- Anisotropic etching process.
- Preferential etching process.

27. What is Isotropic Etching?

In semiconductor technology **isotropic etching** is non-directional removal of material from a substrate via a chemical process using an etchant substance. The etchant may be a corrosive liquid or a chemically active ionized gas, known as plasma.

28. Define accumulation mode.

The initial distribution of mobile positive holes in a p type silicon substrate of a MOS transistor for a voltage much less than the threshold voltage

29. What is Isolation?

It is a process used to provide electrical isolation between different components and interconnections.

30. Give the different types of CMOS process?

1. P-Well process.
2. N-Well process.
3. Twin-tub process.
4. SOI process.

31. What is Channel-stop Implantation?

In N-Well fabrication, N-Well is protected with the resist material. (Because, it should not be affected during Boron implantation). Then Boron is implanted except N-Well. The above said process is done using photo resist mask. This type of implantation is known as Channel-stop implantation.

32. What is LOCOS?

LOCOS mean Local Oxidation of Silicon. This is one type of oxide construction.

33. What is SWAMI?

SWAMI means Side Wall Masked Isolation. It is used to reduce bird's beak effect.

34. What is LDD?

LDD means Lightly Doped Drain Structures.

It is used for implantation of n- region in N-Well process.

35. What is Twin-tub process? Why it is called so?

Twin-tub process is one of the CMOS technologies. Two wells (the other name for well is Tub) are created in this process. So, because of these two tubs, this process is known as Twin-tub process.

36. What are the steps involved in twin-tub process?
   1.   Tub Formation.
   2.   Thin-oxide Construction.
   3.   Source & Drain Implantation.
   4.   Contact cut definition.
   5.   Metallization.

37. What are the special features of Twin-tub process?

In Twin-tub process, Threshold voltage, body effects of n and p devices are independently optimized.

38. What are the advantages of Twin-tub process?

Advantages of Twin-tub process are:

   1.   Separate optimized wells are available.
   2.   Balanced performance is obtained for n and p transistors.

39. What is SOI? What is the material used as Insulator?

SOI means Silicon-on-Insulator. In this process, a Silicon based transistor is built on an insulating material like Sapphire or SiO_2.

40. What are the advantages and disadvantages of SOI process?

Advantages of SOI process:

   1.   There is no well formation in this process.
   2.   There is no field-Inversion problem.
   3.   There is no body effect problem.

Disadvantages of SOI process:

   1.   It is very difficult to protect inputs in this process.
   2.   Device gain is low.
   3.   The coupling capacitance between wires always exists.

41. What are the advantages of CMOS process?

1.   Low power Dissipation.
2.   High Packing density.
3.   Bi directional capability.
4.   Low Input Impedance.
5.   Low delay Sensitivity to load.

42. What is meant by interconnect? What are the types are of interconnect?

Interconnect means connection between various components in an IC. Types of Inter connect:

1.   Metal Inter connect.
2.   Polysilicon Inter connect.
3.   Local Inter connect.

43. What is the fundamental goal in Device modeling?

To obtain the functional relationship among the terminal electrical variables of the device that is to be modeled.

44. What is demarcation line?

Demarcation line is an imaginary line used in stick diagram, to separate p-MOS and n-MOS transistors. All p-MOS transistors are placed above demarcation line and n-MOS below the demarcation line

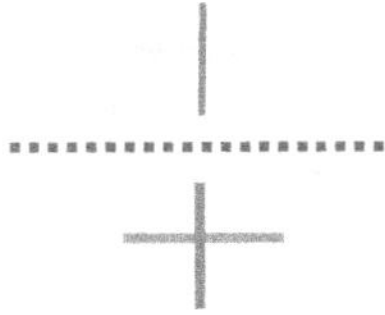

45. What are the two types of Layout design rules?

Lambda design rules and micron rules are major types of layout design rules.

46. What is Silicide?

The combination of Silicon and tantaleum is known as Silicide. It is used as gate material in Polysilicon Interconnect.

47. What is Polycide?

The combination of Silicide and Polysilicon is known as Polycide. It is used as gate material.

48. What is Stick diagram?

The diagram which conveys the layer information through the use of various colours is known as Stick diagram. It is also the cartoon of a chip layout.

49. What are the uses of Stick diagram?

- It can be drawn much easier and faster than a complex layout.
- These are especially important tools for layout built from large cells.

50. Give the various color coding used in stick diagram?

- Green - n-diffusion.
- Red – polysilicon.
- Blue – metal.
- Yellow – implant.
- Black - contact areas.

51. Compare between CMOS and bipolar technologies.

S.No	CMOS Technology	Bipolar Technology
1	High input Impedance	Low input Impedance
2	Low output drive current	High output drive current
3	Low static power dissipation	High power dissipation
4	High packing density	Low packing density
5	Low gm	High gm

52. Define Threshold voltage in CMOS?

The Threshold voltage, VT for a MOS transistor can be defined as the voltage applied between the gate and the source of the MOS transistor below which the drain to source current, IDS effectively drops to zero.

53. What is Body effect?

The threshold voltage Vth is not a constant with respect to the voltage difference between the substrate and the source of MOS transistor. This effect is called substrate-bias effect or body effect.

54. What is Channel-length modulation?

The current between drain and source terminals is constant and independent of the applied voltage over the terminals. This is not entirely correct.

The effective length of the conductive channel is actually modulated by the applied VDS, increasing VDS causes the depletion region at the drain junction to grow, reducing the length of the effective channel.

55. What is Lay-out design rule?

The rules followed to prepare the photo mask are known as Layout design rules.

56. What are LVS and DRL tools?

LVS means Layout Versus Schematic. It checks layout against schematic diagram. It is very important to verify layout.DRC means Design Rule Checker. This tool checks every occurrence of design rule list on layout. Width, spacing of every metal line in layout are checked with this tool.

57. What is hot electron?

Hot electron means because of temperature or any other effects. The electrons or holes jump from channel region to gate oxide region this is called hot electron effect

58. How to avoid the hot electron effect?

We have to keep diode in reverse bias at gate terminal to avoid hot electron effect.

59. In saturation region, what are the factors that affect I_{ds}?

1. Distance between source and drain.
2. Channel width.
3. Threshold voltage.
4. Thickness of oxide layer.
5. Dielectric constant of gate insulator.
6. Carrier mobility.

60. What is Field Oxide?

The thin oxide region is also known as diffusion region. The **field oxide** region is also called the thick oxide region.

61. Give some of the important CAD tools.

Some of the important CAD tools are:

1. Layout editors.
2. Design Rule checkers (DRC).
3. Circuit extraction.

62. What are design rules?

Design rules are the communication link between the designer specifying requirements and the fabricator who materializes them.

Design rules are used to produce workable mask layouts from which the various layers in silicon will be formed or patterned.

63. Define body effect or substrate bias effect.

The threshold voltage Vt is not a constant with respect to the voltage difference between the substrate and the source of the MOS transistor. This effect is called the body effect or substrate bias effect.

Question Bank

Part-A

1. What are four generations of Integration Circuits?
2. Give the advantages of IC?
3. Give the variety of Integrated Circuits?
4. Give the basic process for IC fabrication.
5. What are the various steps for Silicon wafer Preparation?
6. What are the different types of oxidation?
7. What is meant by Latch-up?
8. What is Enhancement mode transistor?
9. What is Depletion mode Device?
10. When the channel is said to be pinched–off?
11. Give the different types of CMOS process?
12. What are the steps involved in twin-tub process?
13. What are the advantages of Silicon-on-Insulator process?
14. What are the advantages of CMOS process?
15. What is the fundamental goal in Device modeling?
16. Define Short Channel devices?
17. Give some of the important CAD tools.
18. What is pull down device?
19. What is pull up device?
20. Why NMOS technology is preferred more than PMOS technology?
21. What are the different operating regions for a MOS transistor?
22. What are the different MOS layers?
23. What is Stick Diagram?
24. What are the uses of Stick diagram?
25. Give the various color coding used in stick diagram?
26. Compare between CMOS and bipolar technologies.
27. Define Threshold voltage in CMOS?
28. What is Body effect?
29. What is Channel-length modulation?
30. Give the basic inverter circuit.
31. Give the CMOS inverter DC transfer characteristics and operating regions
32. What are two components of Power dissipation?

Part-B

1. Describe with neat diagrams the various CMOS fabrication technology.
2. Explain the latch up prevention techniques.
3. Discuss the NMOS fabrication process.
4. Explain the design hierarchies.
5. Enumerate the operation of NMOS Enhancement transistor.
6. Explain about the various non ideal conditions in MOS device model.
7. Derive the CMOS inverter DC characteristics and obtain the relationship for output voltage at different region in the transfer characteristics.
8. Elaborate the operation of PMOS Enhancement transistor.
9. Explain the concept of MOSFET as switches.

CHAPTER 2

COMBINATIONAL LOGIC CIRCUITS

In combinational circuits the output depends on the present input. Half adder is a combinational logic circuit with two inputs and two outputs. The half adder circuit is designed to add two single bit binary number A and B. It is the basic building block for addition of two single bit numbers. This circuit has two outputs carry and sum.

Input		Output	
A	B	S	C
0	0	0	0
0	1	1	0
1	0	1	0
1	1	0	1

a). Truth Table

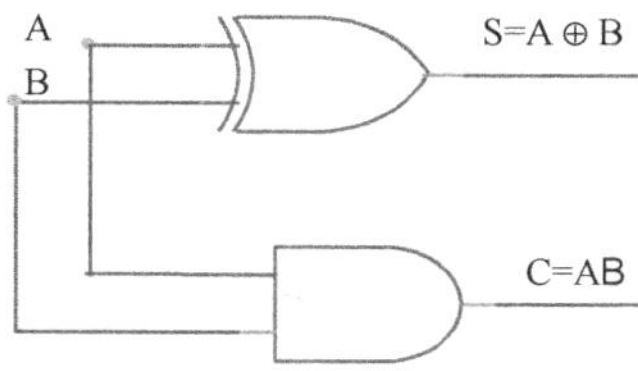

b). Circuit Diagram

Figure 2.1: Half Adder

Full Adder

Full adder can add two one-bit numbers A and B with carry c. The full adder is a three input and two output combinational circuit.

A	B	C_{in}	S	C_{out}
0	0	0	0	0
0	0	1	1	0
0	1	0	1	0
0	1	1	0	1
1	0	0	1	0
1	0	1	0	1
1	1	0	0	1
1	1	1	1	1

a). Truth Table

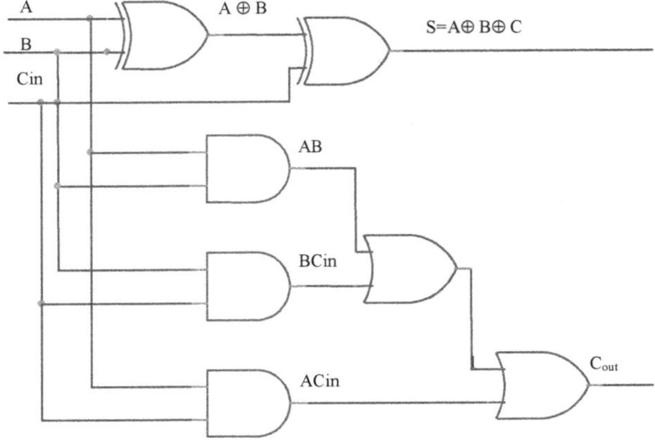

b). Circuit Diagram

Figure 2.2: Full Adder

4x1Mux

Multiplexer is a special type of combinational circuit. There are n-data inputs, one output and m select inputs with $2^m = n$. It is a digital circuit which selects one of the n data inputs and routes it to the output. The selection of one of the n inputs is done by the selection inputs. Depending on the selection inputs one out of n data inputs is selected and transmitted to the single output Y.

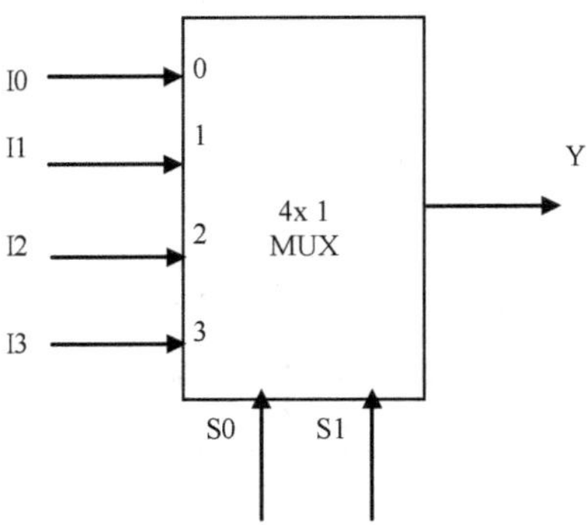

a). Block Diagram

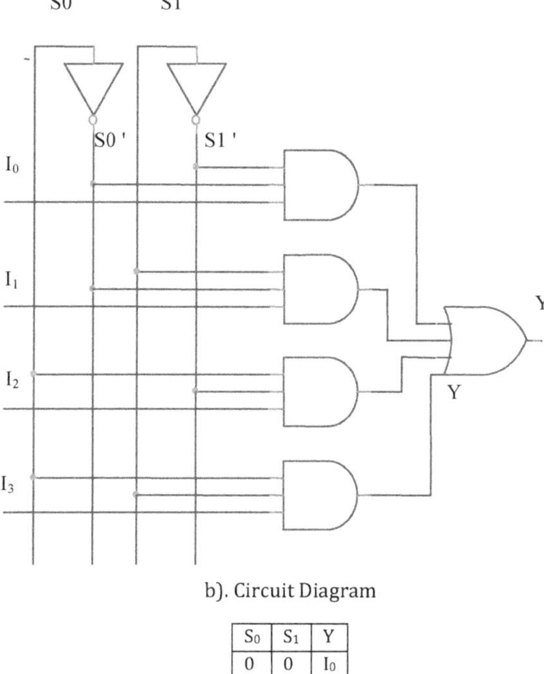

b). Circuit Diagram

S₀	S₁	Y
0	0	I₀
0	1	I₁
1	0	I₂
1	1	I₃

c). Truth Table

Figure 2.3: 4x1MUX

2.1.   Delay Estimation

The response of the circuit depends on the delays produced by the circuit elements. So a model to accurately predict the delay time is necessary.

2.1.1.   RC Delay Model

MOS transistors can be approximated as a switch in series with resistor. NMOS gate and diffusion terminals have parasitic capacitance. This RC effect can be modeled and used to calculate delay of logic gates. If the logic gates use minimum length devices, then the time delay, power and area is reduced.

Elmore Delay Model

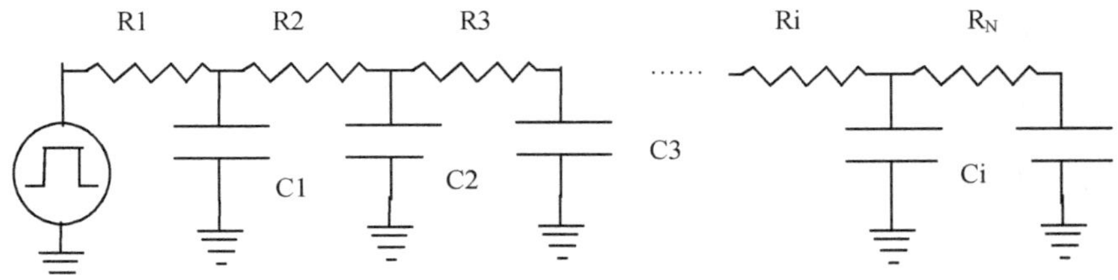

Figure 2.4: RC Network for Calculation of Delay

The transistor in ON condition is replaced by resistor. In linear region, current Ids is proportional to Vds

$$Rd = \frac{\Delta vds}{\Delta Ids}$$

The delay introduced by RC ladder using Elmore delay model is given by

$$= \sum_{i=1}^{N} Ci \sum_{j=1}^{i} Rj = \sum_{i=1}^{N} Ci \; Rii$$

Where Rii is the path resistance.

As W increases resistance R decreases but capacitance C increases. Capacitance directly affects the speed.

$$\text{Time delay } \zeta = RC$$

Consider a resistor capacitor network with following assumptions.

1. The network has single input node.
2. All capacitors are between node and ground.
3. The network does not contain any resistive loops.

Unique resistance path exists between source node S and any node i of the network. Total resistance along this path is called path resistance.

Path resistance between S and node4 is given by R44

$$R44 = R1 + R3 + R4.$$

Rik= Resistance shared by among the paths from root node S to node **k** and **i**.

$$Rik = \sum Rj = (Rj \in [\text{path}(s \rightarrow i) \cap \text{path}(s \rightarrow k)])$$

$$Ri4 = R1+R3 \qquad\qquad Ri2 = R1$$

Initially N nodes of the network are discharged to GND.

$$\zeta = \sum_{k=1}^{N} Ck\ Rik$$

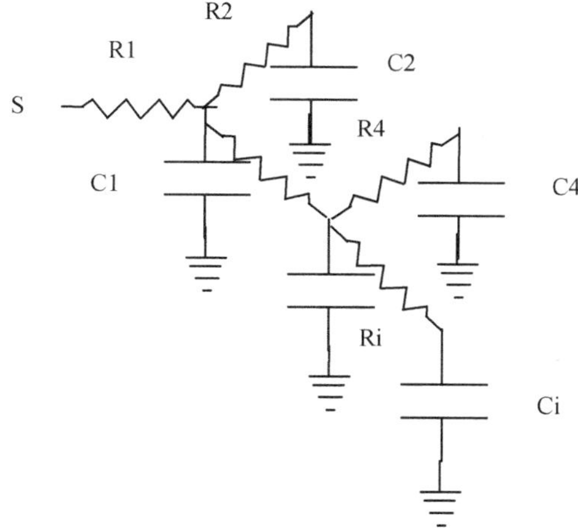

Figure 2.5: Network for Calculation of Delay

For the above Network

$$\zeta = R1\ C1 + R1\ C2 + (R1+R3)\ C3 + (R1+R4)\ C4 + (R1+R3+Ri)\ Ci$$

2.1.2. *Linear Delay Model*

In linear delay model propagation delay is the sum of parasitic delay inherent to the gate and effort delay.

Propagation delay d = p + f

The relation f d = g h exists.

Where g = Logical effort.

h = fan out or electrical effort.

$$h = \frac{cout}{cin}$$

A logic gate has one or more inputs and output, subject to the following restrictions: The gate of each transistor is connected to an input a power supply or the output and inputs are connected only to transistor gates.

Logical effort (g) of a gate is defined as the ratio of the input capacitance of the gate to the input capacitance of an inverter that can deliver the same output current.

2.1.3. *Parasitic Delay (p)*

It is the delay of the gate when it drives zero load. It can be calculation by RC model. A simple method of calculation is to count only diffusion capacitance on the output node. For gates with 1 input parasitic delay is 1. Similarly for 2 inputs gate parasitic delay are 2.

Fan in: Fan in of a logic gate is the number of inputs the gate has in the logic path being exercised.

Fan out: Fan out of logic gate total number of gate inputs that are driven by gate output.

Table 2.1: Parasitic Delay of Gates

Gate Type	No. of inputs			
	1	2	3	n
INVERTER	1			
NAND		2	3	
NOR		2	3	

2.2. Static CMOS Design

Complementary MOS is one static circuit in which at every point of time each gate output is connected to either VDD or VSS via low resistance path output of the gates. Static CMOS circuit with complementary NMOS pull down and PMOS pull up networks are used for majority of logic gates in IC. They have good noise margins and are fast.

Advantages

1. Good noise margin.
2. Low power.
3. Insensitive to device variations.
4. Easy to design.
5. Available in standard cell libraries.

AND and OR functions are derived from NAND and NOR.

$$\overline{Ao + A1} \ = \ \overline{Ao} . \ \overline{A1}$$

$$\overline{Ao \bullet A1} \ = \ \overline{Ao} + \overline{A1}$$

Function F = $\overline{AB + CD}$ can be computed with an AND-OR-INVERT.

2.2.1. Complementary CMOS

Static CMOS gate is combination of two networks.

1. Pull up Network (PUN).
2. Pull down Network (PDN).

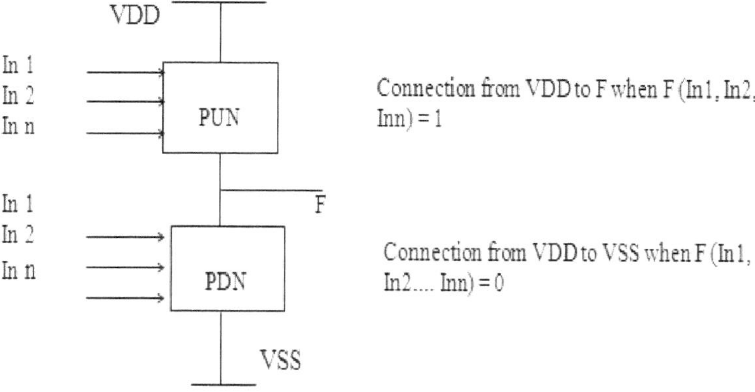

Figure 2.6: Complementary CMOS

Function of PUN is to provide connection between output and VDD when output of logic gate is 1.

Function PUN is to connect output to Vss when output of logic gate is o PUN and PDN are constructed in mutually exclusive fashion such that only one network is conducting in steady state.

A path always exists between VDD and output F for 1 or between Vss and F for output 0.

Constructing PDN & PUN

CMOS act as switch controlled by gate signal. PDN is constructed using NMOS Devices and PUN is constructed using PMOS Devices because NMOS gives strong zeros and PMOS gives strong ones.

Example

1. Implement 2 input NAND gate using Static CMOS.

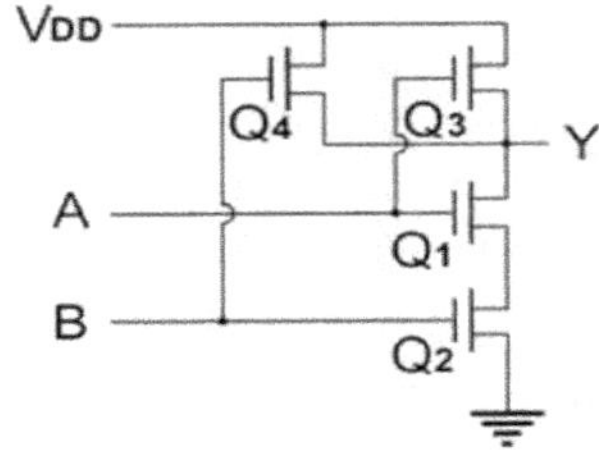

2. Implement f= $\overline{AB+C}$

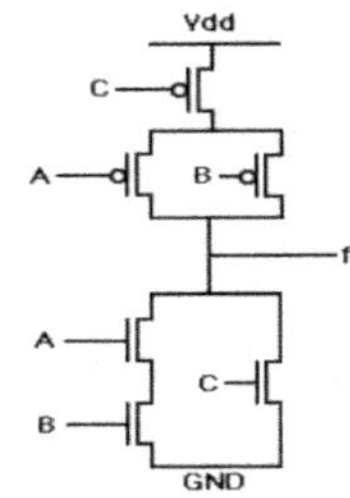

3. Implement 2 input NOR gate using static CMOS

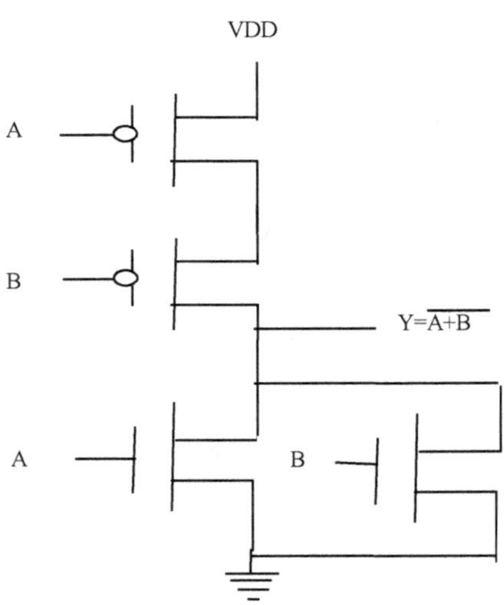

4. Implement Y= $\overline{AB+CD}$ using static CMOS

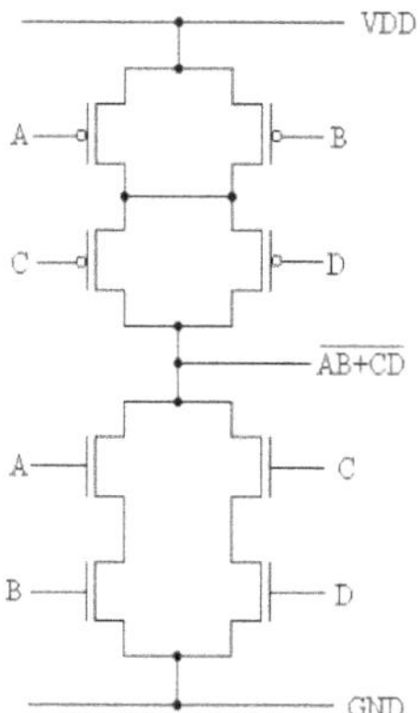

Static Properties of Complementary CMOS

1. No static power dissipation between PUN & PDN because both are mutually exclusive.

2.3.   Ratioed Logic

To reduce the number of transistors required to implement a given logic function at the cost of reduced power dissipation. The purpose of PUN in to provide conditional path between VDD & output when PDN is OFF. PUN can be replaced by load that did the same function. PMOS load with ground is known as pseudo NMOS gate. Voltage swing on output & overall functioning of gate depends on the ratio is NMOS and PMOS sizes. So the circuit is called rationed logic.

Pseudo-NMOS Circuits

Static CMOS gates are slowed because an input must drive both NMOS and PMOS transistors. In any transition, either the pull up or pull down network is activated; meaning that capacitance of the inactive network loads the input. Moreover, PMOS transistors have poor mobility and must be sized larger to achieve comparable rising and falling delays.

Pseudo-NMOS and dynamic gates offer improved speed by removing the PMOS transistors form loading the input, this section analyzes pseudo-NMOS gates, while section explores dynamic logic. Pseudo-NMOS gates resemble static gates, but replace the slow PMOS pull up with a single grounded PMOS transistor which acts as a pull up resistor. The pull up resistance should be large enough that the NMOS transistors can pull the output ground, yet low enough to rapidly pull the output high. The following figure shows several Pseudo gates ratioed such that the pull down transistor is about four times as strong as the pull up.

When PDN is OFF and PUN is ON, then VOH is equal to VDD and VOL is not equal to 0v.Since there is a contention between devices in PDN & grounded PMOS load device. This reduces noise margin and static power dissipation.

Advantages of Pseudo NMOS

1. It uses reduced number of transistors

If N is number of inputs, then transistors needed is reduced to N+1 but for complementary CMOS, 2N transistors are required.

Example

1. Implement the function $y = \overline{A + B}$ using pseudo CMOS.

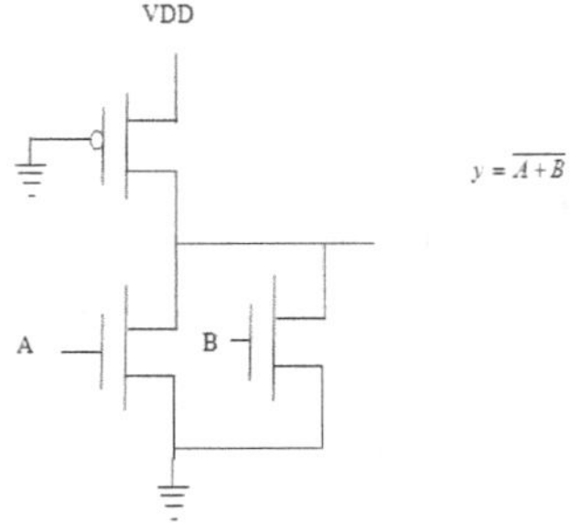

2. $y = \overline{A}$ using pseudo NMOS

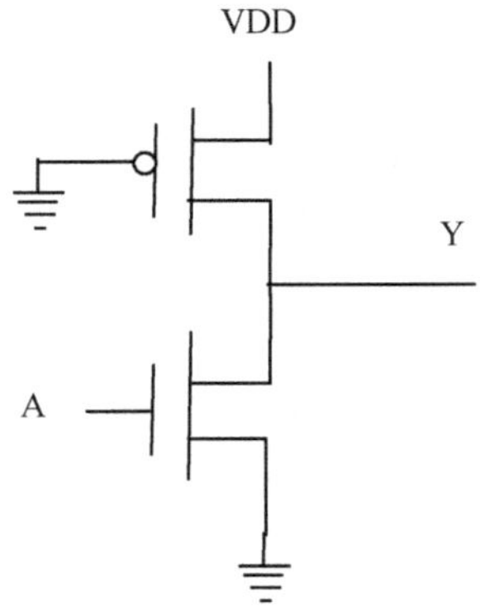

2.4.   Ganged CMOS

Pair of CMOS inverters ganged together is called Ganged CMOS. The circuit for computation of a NOR function is given below.

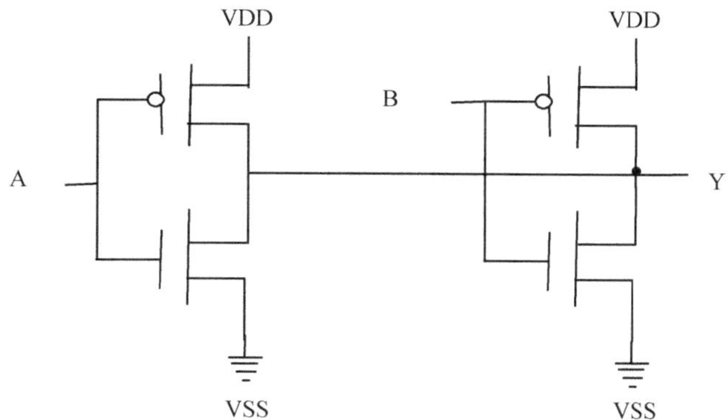

Figure 2.7: Ganged CMOS Implementation of NOR

2.5.   Cascade Voltage Switch Logic (CVSL)

It uses both true and complementary input signals and computes both true and complementary automatic a part of NMOS and pull-down networks.

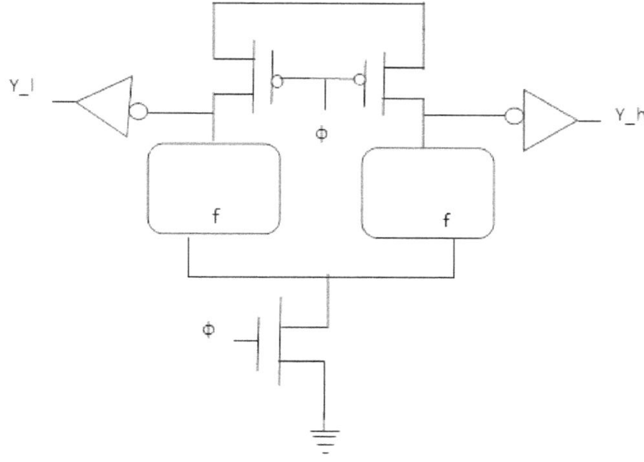

Figure 2.8: Cascade Voltage Switch Logic

The pull down network F implements the logic function as in static CMOS gate for given input one of pull down networks will be ON and the OFF. The pull down network that is ON will pull that output low. This low output turns ON the PMOS transistor to pull the opposite output high. When the opposite output rises, the other PMOS transistor turns OFF so no static power dissipation occurs.

2.6.   Dynamic CMOS Design

Pseudo NMOS uses N+1 transistor to implement N input logic gates but has static power dissipation. Dynamic logic is introduced with addition of clock input. It works in precharge and Evaluation phase. PDN is constructed as in complementary CMOS.

2.6.1. Dynamic CMOS

Dynamic circuits relies on temporary storage of signal values on capacitance of high impedances circuit nodes. Resulting gate structure is simple & faster. But it fails because of increased sensitivity to noise.

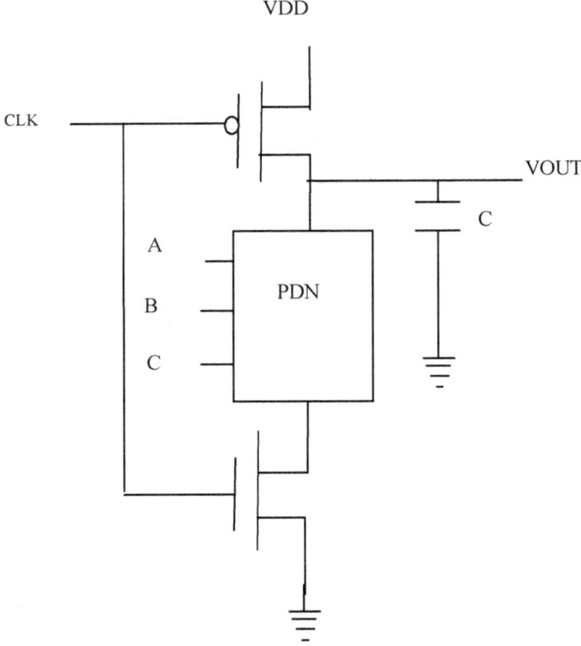

Figure 2.9: Structure of Dynamic CMOS

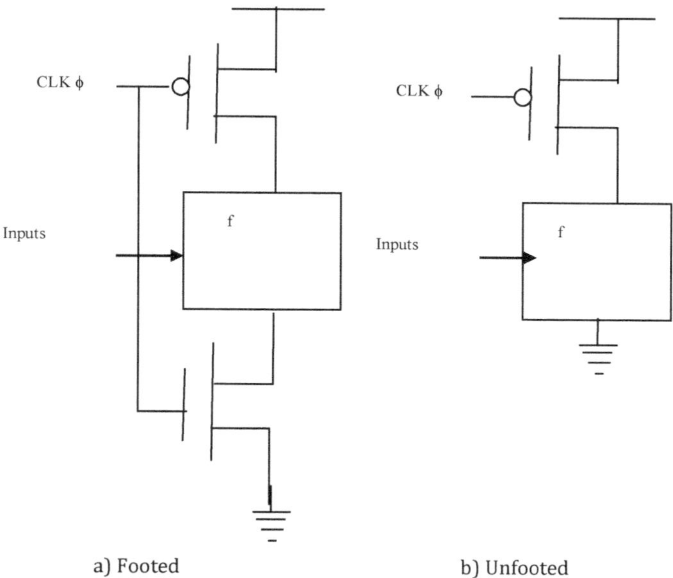

a) Footed   b) Unfooted

Figure 2.10: Footed and Un Footed Implementation of Dynamic Logic

The operation of dynamic CMOS structure in Precharge and Evaluation is given below.

Precharge

When clock φ=o, the output is precharged to VDD by PMOS transistor. At that time the NMOS transistor is off so PDN is disabled. Evaluation FET ie NMOS eliminates static power during precharge period.

Evaluation

When input=1, the transistor PMOS is off and NMOS is on and output is discharged based on input values and PDN. Then low resistance path exists between output and GND. The output is discharged to GND.

Precharge values are stored in output capacitance CL. The capacitance values include junction capacitance, wire capacitances & capacitance of fanout gates. During this phase ,there is only one path between output and supply. Once output is discharged, it cannot be charged again until precharge takes place. Output goes to high impedance state during evaluation period if PDN = OFF.

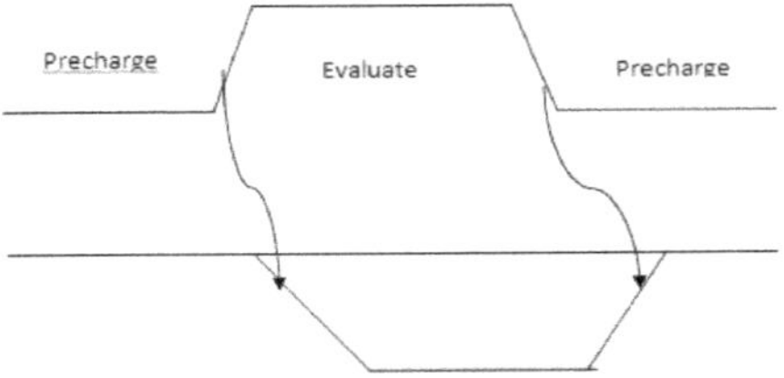

Figure 2.11: Timing Diagram of Dynamic Circuit

Dynamic gates offer even better logical effort and lower power consumption by using a precharge transistor instead of a pull up that is always conducting. Unfortunately, if one dynamic inverter directly drives another, a race can corrupt the result.

Properties of Dynamic Logic

1. Logic function implemented by NMOS PDN is same as static CMOS.
2. No ÷ of transistors is lower ie N+2 instead of 2N.
3. It consumes dynamic power. No static current.
4. Faster switching speed.

Problem in Cascading Dynamic Circuits

The HIGH input to the first gate causes its output to fall, but the second gate falls in response to its initial HIGH input. The circuit therefore produces an incorrect result the second output will never rise during evaluation. Domino circuits solve this problem by using inverting static gates between dynamic gates so that the input to each dynamic gate is initially LOW.

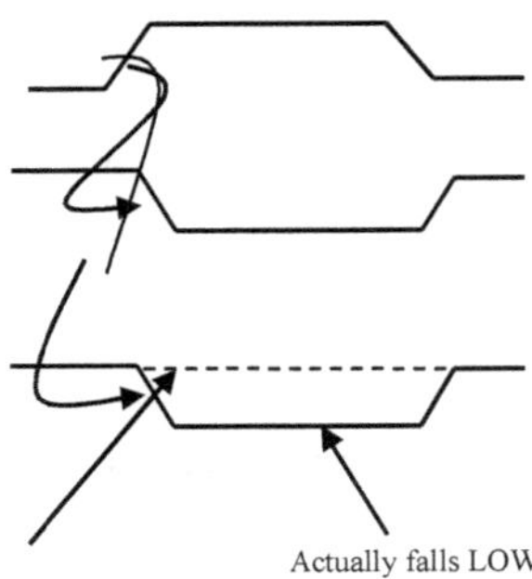

Figure 2.12: Problem in Cascading Dynamic Circuits

Example

1.   Implement Z= $\overline{(A+B)}C$ and Y= $\overline{ABC}$ using static CMOS

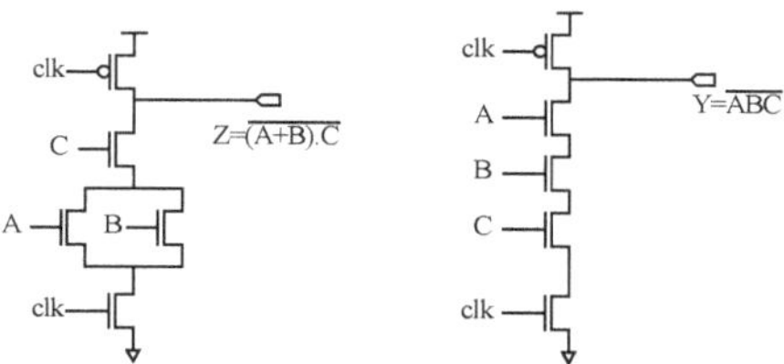

2.6.2. *Domino Logic*

It is an extension of dynamic logic circuit by adding an inverter at the output to overcome the glitch. Pseudo-NMOS gates eliminate the bulky PMOS transistors loading the inputs, but price of quiescent power dissipation and contention between the pull up and pull down transistors.

Important feature of Domino Logic is

1.   They have smaller area than conventional CMOS logic.
2.   Parasitic capacitances are smaller so that higher operating speeds are possible.
3.   Operation is free of glitches as each gate can make only one transition.
4.   Only non-inverting structures are possible because of the presence of inverting buffer.
5.   Charge sharing is a problem.

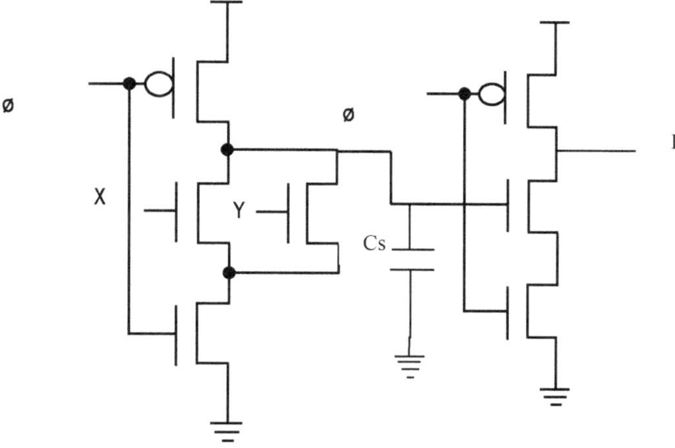

Figure 2.13: Structure of 2 Input OR Gate Domino Logic

Here Cs precharges to a value Vs = VDD, which gives F =0. During Evaluation NMOS array discharges Cs to a voltage of Vs = 0v, which changes the output F = VDD. ie '1' state.

2.6.3. NP Domino

The structure of NP Domino is shown below.

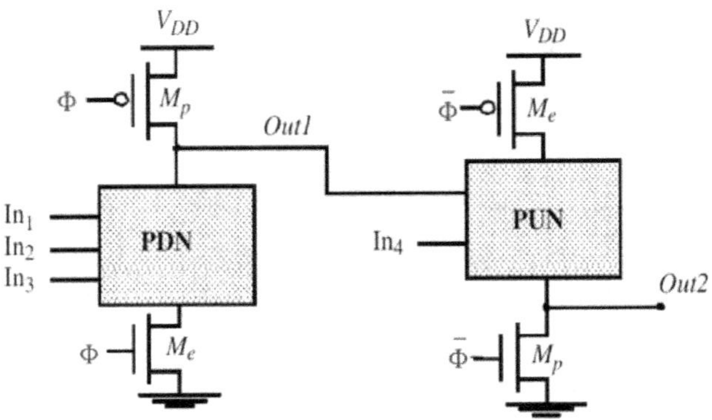

Figure 2.14: Structure of NP Domino

2.6.4. Dual Rail Domino

Dual functions can be implemented by using dual rail domino structure.

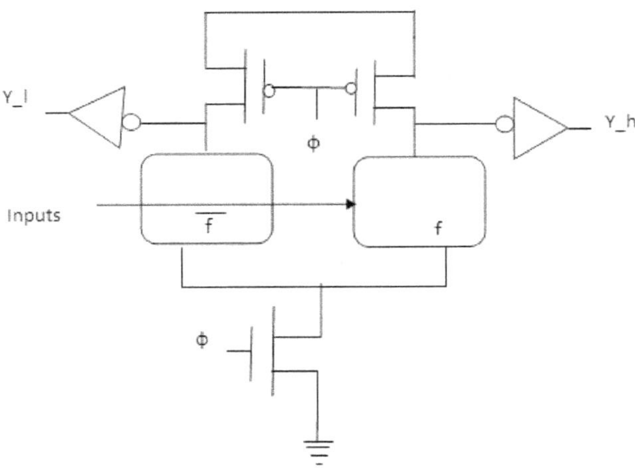

Figure 2.15: Dual Rail Domino Structure

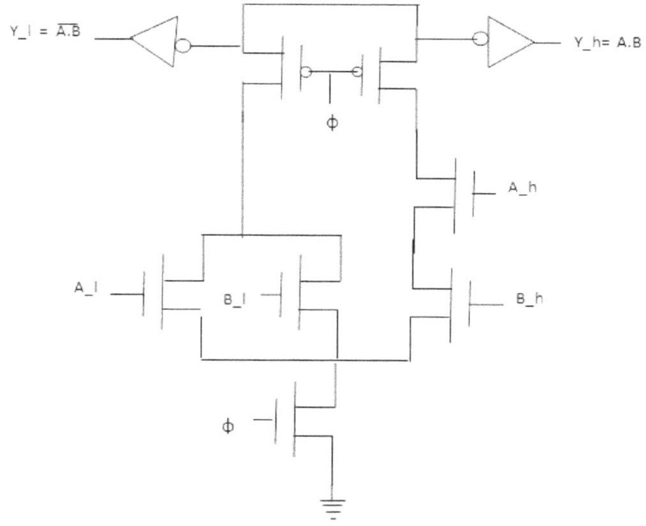

Figure 2.16: Dual Rail Domino AND/NAND

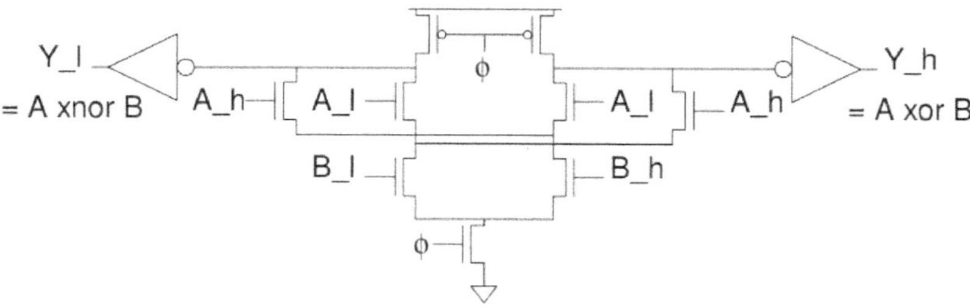

Figure 2.17: Dual Rail Domino NOR/ XNOR

2.6.5. *Self-Resetting Logic (SR Logic)*

It uses a feedback network to automatically restore the charge on the internal capacitor after a discharge. One PMOS has been added for the construction of SR latch. The function F output is connected to the gate of self-Resetting transistor through inverter.

A precharge with ϕ=0 charges C_s to the value Vs = VDD. As the result F=0 self resetting transistor M_R is OFF. When the clock changes to ϕ=1, a discharge event makes Vs=0v. This causes F=1, which fed to the gate of M_R through the chain of inverters. M_R turns on and recharges the node voltage Vs = VDD.

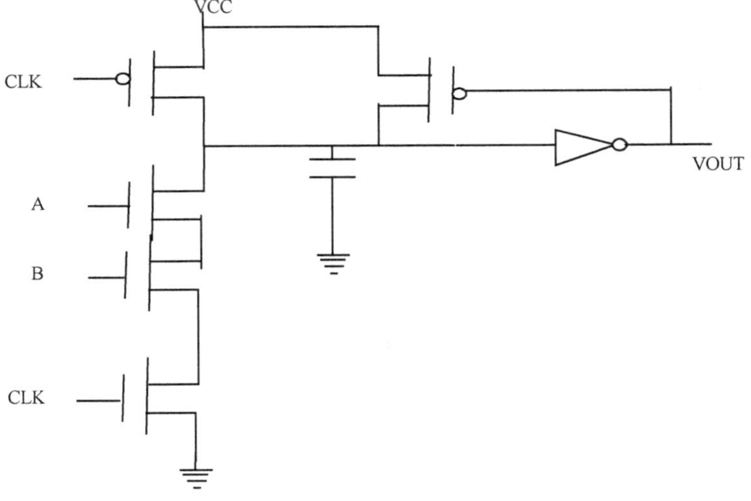

Figure 2.18: Self Resetting Logic

2.7.   Transmission Gate

It is formed by a combination of NMOS and PMOS . NMOS and PMOS is placed parallel in transmission Gate. Symbol and switching model of Transmission gate is given below. NMOS, PMOS and CMOS transmission gate can be used to steer or transfer charge from one node of a circuit to another node under the control of MOSFET gate voltage.

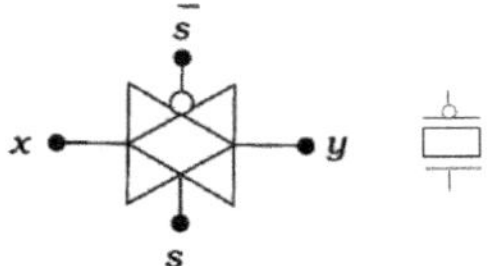

Figure 2.19: Symbol of Transmission Gate

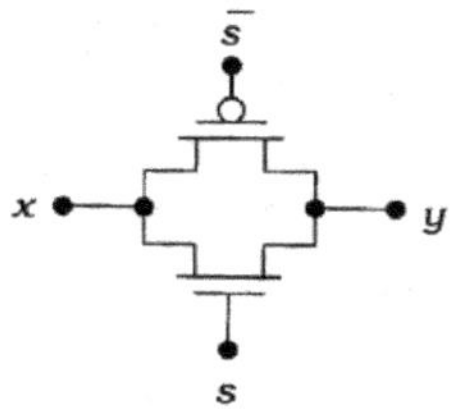

Figure 2.20: Equivalent Circuit of Transmission Gate

When, s=1, both PMOS & NMOS are on and output follows input. When s=0 both are off and the output remains same.

Applications of Transmission Gate are

1. Multiplexer.
2. Latch.
3. Analog switch.

Disadvantages of CMOS Transmission Gate Compared with Pass Transistor

1. It requires more Area.
2. It need complemented control signals.

MUX using TG

It selects either input A or B on the basis of control signal.

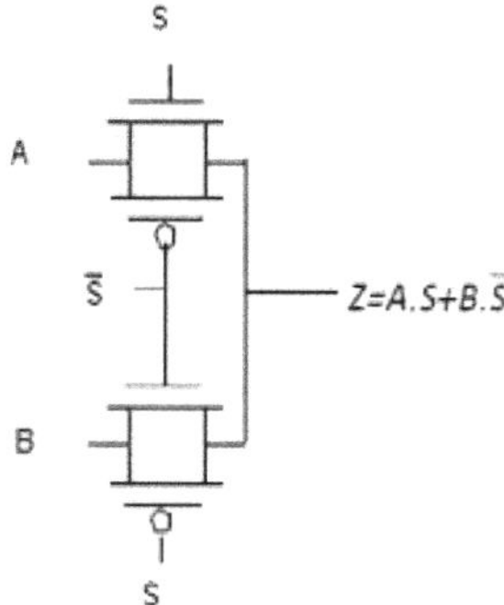

Figure 2.21: 2*1 Mux Using Transmission Gate

2.8.   Pass Transistor Logic

Pass Transistor Using NMOS

Assume that in NMOS both gate and drain voltage are at 0v. When gate voltage is changed to 5v and transistor turns on and drives source towards Vdd. When source voltage increases, vgs decreases below vtn.

When Vs = 0 the voltage Vgs > Vtn. Now the transistor is ON and current flows. If the source voltage rises to Vs=VDD-Vtn, Vgs falls to Vtn and transistor is cut off. So NMOS transistor passes '0' well but '1' poorly.

When VD = 5V;   Vout = 5 - Vtn.

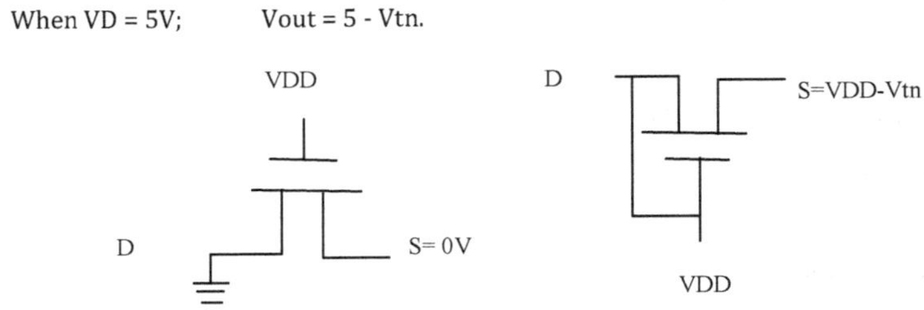

Figure 2.22: Pass Transistor Using NMOS

Pass Transistor Using PMOS

PMOS initially assumes Vg and Vs are at 5v. When we change Vg to 0v then transistor turns on and drives source voltage towards 0v.When Vs is decreased to Vt, the transistor turns off. Hence steady state voltage is equal to Vt.

When the PMOS Gate and Drain are connected to GND then Vs = |Vtp|. If the source voltage drops below |Vtp| , then the transistor is cut off.

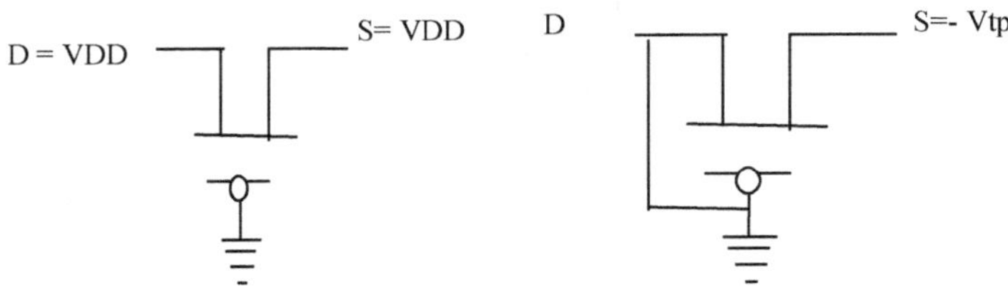

Figure 2.23: Pass Transistor Using PMOS

Table 2.2: Different Signal Voltages

Signal	Voltage(V)
Strong one	4.5 V-5.0V
Weak one	3.5 V-4.5V
Strong zero	0-0.5V
Weak zero	0.5-1.5V

Advantages of Pass Transistor over Standard NMOS

1. They are 'ratioed' devices and of minimum Geometry.
2. They do not have a path from VDD to VSS. So do not dissipate power in 'stand by' Condition.

Example

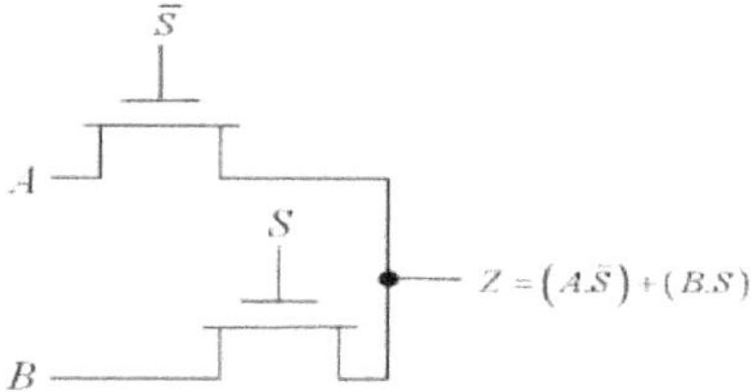

Figure 2.24: 2*1 MUX Using Pass Transistor

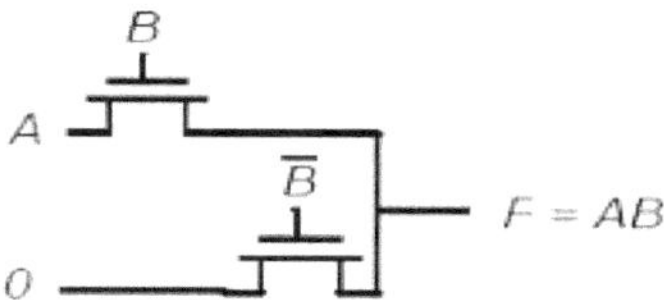

Figure 2.25: AND Gate Using Pass Transistor

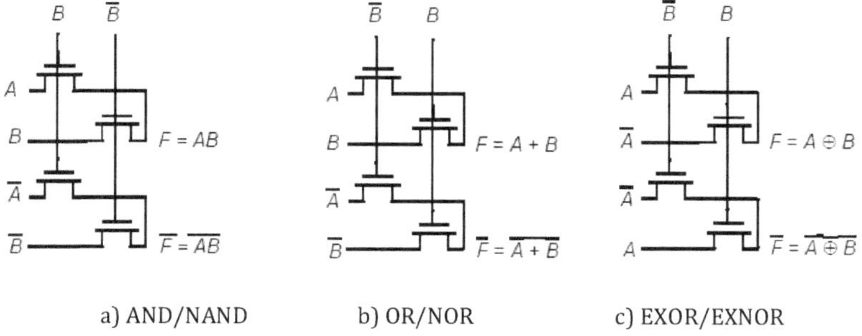

a) AND/NAND   b) OR/NOR   c) EXOR/EXNOR

Figure 2.26: Pass Transistor Implementation

2.9. Power Dissipation

There are two components that are responsible for power dissipation. They are:

1. Static dissipation due to leakage current or other current drawn continuously from the power supply.
2. Dynamic dissipation due to.
   - Switching transient current.
   - Charging and discharging of load capacitances.

$$P_{total} = P_{static} + P_{dynamic}$$

2.9.1. *Static Power Dissipation*

It occurs due to leakage current continuously drawn from power supply.

Instantaneous power P(t) drawn from power supply is proportional to supply current i_{DD} (t) & voltage V_{DD}

$$P(t) = i_{DD}(t). VDD$$

Average Power (Pavg)

The average power is given by,

$$Pavg = \frac{E}{T} = \frac{1}{T} \int_{o}^{T} i_{DD}(t). VDD \, dt$$

Static power dissipation occurs due to sub threshold conduction. Parasitic diodes exist between P-Well & N-Well with substrate. Such parasitic diodes are reverse biased; their leakage current contributes to static power dissipation.

$$Io = Is \left(e^{\frac{qv}{kT}} - 1 \right)$$

$$Pstatic = \sum_{1}^{n} \text{Leakage current} * \text{supply voltages}$$

Where n = Number of devices

Leakage current ranges from 0.1 nA to 0.5 nA. Static power dissipation due to leakage for an inverter operating 5v is between 1 and 2 nw.

2.9.2. *Dynamic Power Dissipation*

- It occurs during input transition from '0' to 1 or from '1' to '0'. Both NMOS and PMOS transistors ON for a short period of time during the transition. This results in a short current pulse from VDD to VSS. It is called short circuit current dissipation.

- Current is required to charge and discharge the output capacitance load. The current pulse from VDD to VSS results in a short-circuit. Dissipation is dependent on the input rise/fall time and load capacitance.

As the capacitive load is increased, the charge or discharge current dominates. The average dynamic power dissipation during switching of square wave is given by,

$$P \, dyn = \frac{1}{T} \int_{o}^{T/2} in(t) \, . \, Vout \, dt + \frac{1}{T} \int_{T/2}^{T} i_{p}(t) \, (VDD \, Vout) \, dt$$

$$f \, (\text{Repetition frequency}) = \frac{1}{T}$$

i_n = NMOS transient current

i_p = PMOS transient current

As f=10 MHZ the advantages of CMOS vanishes, both NMOS & CMOS consumes same power. Current spike occurs for each switching.

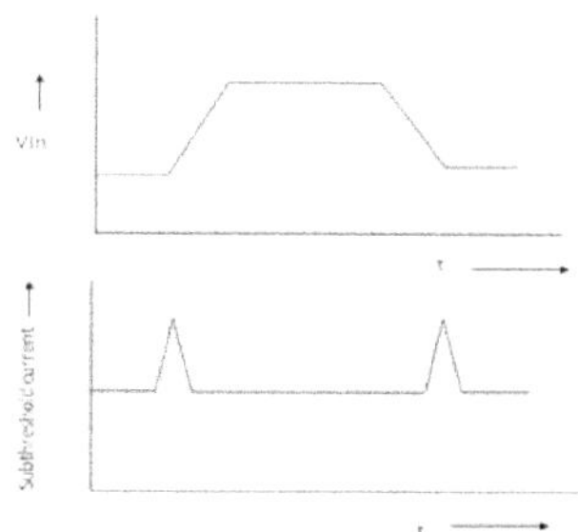

Figure 2.27: Leakage Current

For a step input.

$$i_n(t) = CL \frac{dvout}{dt}$$

C_L = load capacitance

$$Pd = \frac{C_L}{T} \int_{o}^{VDD} vout \; dout + \frac{CL}{T} \int_{VDD}^{o} (VDD - vout) \; d(VDD - Vout)$$

$$Pd = \frac{CL}{T} [(vout)^2 / 2]_{o}^{VDD} + \frac{CL}{T} [(VDD - vout)^2 / 2]_{VDD}^{o}$$

$$Pd = \frac{CL}{2T} VDD^2 + \frac{CL}{2T} \cdot VDD^2 - \frac{CL}{T} 0 = \frac{CL}{T} VDD^2$$

Substituting $T = \dfrac{1}{f}$.

$$Pd = CL \cdot f \, VDD^2$$

$$Psc = \frac{\beta}{12} (VDD^{-2vt})^3 \frac{trf}{tp}$$

Where tp is the period of wave form

$$trf = tr = tf$$

$$\boxed{P_{total} = Ps + Pd + P_{sc}}$$

2.10. Power Minimization

- DC power dissipation may be reduced to leakage by using complementary logic gates.
- Device with minimum size reduces power.
- Dynamic power dissipation may be limited by supply voltage, switched capacitance and frequency at which logic is clocked.

2.10.1. Dynamic Power Reduction

If the process is selected with high threshold voltages and oxide thickness, dynamic power dissipation dominates. The dynamic power is reduced by decreasing switching capacitance, power supply or the operating frequency. Switching capacitance is reduced by choosing small transistors. Interconnect switching capacitances is most affectedly reduced through careful floor planning.   Choosing a low power supply significantly reduces power consumption. Low power system uses 1.5V-3V supplies.

2.10.2. Static Power Reduction

- Reducing Ista reduces static power.

Sub threshold leakage power is a major problem.

One method of reducing leakage current low power system is to turn off the power supply entirely. This could be done internally with a series transistor. Multiple threshold CMOS circuits use low Vt transistors for computation and Vt.transistor as a switch to disconnect power supply during idle mode.

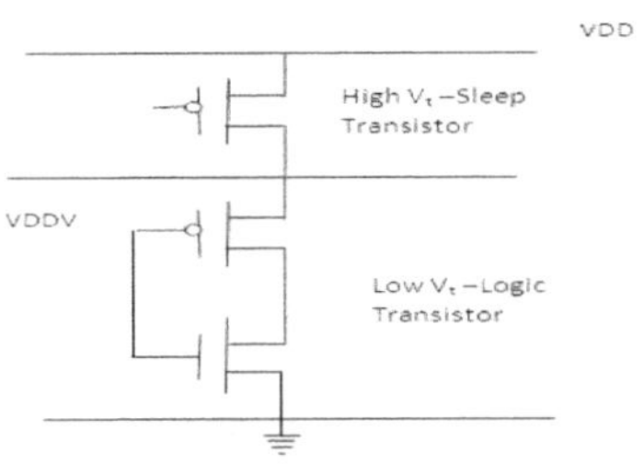

Figure 2.28: Circuit Showing the use of Low and High Vt Transistor for Power Reduction

- SOI circuits consume less leakage current. Switched capacitance includes gate capacitance, diffusion capacitance and wire capacitance.
- Good floor planning reduces the long wires in a system.
- Good layout minimizes the size of diffusion region for particular gate width.

2 Marks with Answer

1. Define Elmore delay model?

It is an analytical method used to estimate the RC delay in a network. Elmore delay model estimates the delay of a RC ladder as the sum over each node in the ladder of the resistance Rn-between that node and a supply multiplied by the capacitor on the nodes.

2. What are the general properties of Elmore delay model?

General property of Elmore delay model network has

- Single input node.
- All the capacitors are between a node and ground Network does not contain any resistive loop.

3. What are the types of power dissipation?

- Static power dissipation (due to leakage current when the circuit is idle).
- Dynamic power dissipation (when the circuit is switching).
- Short –circuit power dissipation during switching of transistors.

4. What is static power dissipation?

Power dissipation due to leakage current when the idle is called the static power dissipation. Static power is due to Sub threshold conduction through OFF transistors, Tunneling current through gate oxide, Leakage through reverse biased diodes and contention current in radioed circuits.

5. What is Dynamic power dissipation?

Power dissipation is due to circuit switching to charge and discharge the output load capacitance at a particular node at operating frequency is called Dynamic power dissipation. The Dynamic power dissipation at a particular output node is given by,

$$Pd = CL \; Vdd^2 \; f.$$

Where, CL = load capacitance

Vdd = power supply

f = operating frequency

6. What are the methods to reduce dynamic power dissipation?

1. Reducing the product of capacitance and its switching frequency .
2. Eliminate logic switching that is not necessary for computation.
3. Reduce activity factor Reduce supply voltage

7. What are the methods to reduce static power dissipation?

1. By selecting multi threshold voltages on circuit paths with low-Vt transistors while leakage on other paths with high-Vt transistors.

2. By using two operating modes, active and standby for each function blocks.

3. By adjusting the body bias (i.e) adjusting FBB (Forward Body Bias) in active mode to increase performance and RBB (Reverse Body Bias) in standby mode to reduce leakage.

4. By using sleep transistors to isolate the supply from the block to achieve significant leakage power savings.

8. What is short circuit power dissipation?

During switching, both NMOS and PMOS transistors will conduct simultaneously and provide a direct path between Vdd and the ground rail resulting in short circuit power dissipation

9. Define design margin?

The additional performance capability above required standard basic system parameters that may be specified by a system designer to compensate for uncertainties is called design margin. Design margin required as there are three sources of variation- two environmental and one manufacturing.

10. Write the applications of transmission gate?

- Multiplexing element of path selector.
- A latch element.
- An unlock switch.
- Act as a voltage controlled resistor connecting the input and output.

11. What is pass transistor?

It is a MOS transistor, in which gate is driven by a control signal the source (out), the drain of the transistor is called constant or variable voltage potential (in). If the control signal is high, input is passed to the output and when the control signal is low, the output is in floating topology .

12. List the advantages of pass transistor?

Pass transistor logic (PTL) circuits are often superior to standard CMOS circuits in terms of layout density, circuit delay and power consumption. They do not have path VDD to GND and do not dissipate standby power (static power dissipation).

13. What is transmission gate?

The circuit constructed with the parallel connection of PMOS and NMOS with shorted drain and source terminals. The gate terminal uses two select signals s and s. When **s** is high than the transmission gates pass the signal on the input. The main advantage of transmission gate is that it eliminates the threshold voltage drop.

14. Compare and contrast clock gating versus power gating approaches.

Clock gating minimizes dynamic power by stopping unnecessary transitions, but power gating minimizes leakage power by inserting a high Vt transistor in series with low Vt logic blocks.

15. What are the various ways to reduce the delay time of a CMOS inverter?

Various ways for reducing the delay time are given below:

a) The width of the MOS transistor can be increased to reduce delay. This is known as gate sizing.

b) The load capacitance can be reduced to reduce delay. This is achieved by using transistor with lower size.

c) Delay can also be reduced by increasing the supply voltage Vdd and/or reducing the threshold voltage Vt of the MOS transistors.

16. Explain the basic operation of a 2- phase dynamic circuit

The operation of the circuit can be explained using precharge logic in which the output is precharged to HIGH level during Φ2 clock and the output is evaluated during Φ1 clock.

17. What makes dynamic CMOS circuits faster than static CMOS circuits ?

As MOS dynamic circuits require lesser number of transistors and capacitance is to be driven by it. This makes MOS dynamic circuits faster.

18. What is glitching power dissipation?

Because of finite delay of gates used to realize Boolean functions, different signals cannot reach the inputs of a gate simultaneously. This leads to spurious transition at the output before it settles down to its final value. The spurious transition leads to charging and discharging of the outputs causing glitching power dissipation. It can be minimized by having balanced realization having same delay at the inputs.

19. List various sources of leakage currents?

Various source of leakage currents are listened below:

I1=Reverse-bias p-n junction diode leakage current.

I2=band-to-band tunneling current.

I3=Sub threshold leakage current.

I4=Gate oxide tunneling current.

I5=Gate current due to hot carrier junction.

I6=Channel punch through.

I7=Gate induced drain leakage current.

20. What are the classifications of CMOS circuit families?

- Static CMOS circuits.
- Dynamic CMOS circuits.
- Ratioed circuits.
- Pass-transistor circuits.

21. What is the characteristics of Static CMOS design ?

A static CMOS circuit is a combination of two networks – the pull-up network (PUN) and the pull-down network (PDN) in which at every point in time, each gate output is connected to either VDD or VSS via a low resistance line.

22. List the important properties of Static CMOS design.

At any instant of time, the output of the gate is directly connected to VDD or VSS. The function of the PUN is to provide a connection between the output and VDD. The function of the PDN is provide a connection between the output and VSS .Both PDN and PUN are constructed in mutually exclusive way such that one of the networks is conducting in steady state.

23. What is Dynamic CMOS logic?

Dynamic circuits rely on the temporary storage of signal values on the capacitance of high impedance node. It requires only N+2 transistors. It takes a sequence of precharge and conditional evaluation phases to realizes logic functions.

24. What are the properties of Dynamic logic?

- Logic function is implemented by pull-down network only.
- Full swing outputs (VOL= GND and VOH = VDD).
- Non-ratioed.
- Faster switching speeds.
- Needs a precharge clock.

25. What are the disadvantages of dynamic CMOS technology?

- A fundamental difficulty with dynamic circuits is a loss of noise immunity and a serious timing restriction on the inputs of the gate.
- Violate monotonicity during evaluation phase.

26. What is CMOS Domino logic?

A static CMOS inverter placed between dynamic gates which eliminate the monotonicity problem in dynamic circuits are called CMOS Domino logic.

Question Bank

Part-A

1. Define Rise, fall and delay time.
2. Draw the Dual-Rail Domino Logic Circuits.
3. Write the equation for static and dynamic power.
4. Draw the timing diagram for Domino logic circuits.

Part–B

1. Discuss in detail about the ratioed circuit and dynamic circuit CMOS logic configurations
2. Describe the basic principle of operation of dynamic CMOS, domino and NP domino logic with neat diagrams.
3. Explain the static and dynamic power dissipation in CMOS circuits with necessary diagrams and expressions.
4. Discuss the design techniques to reduce switching activity in a static and dynamic CMOS circuits.
5. Briefly discuss about the classification of circuit families and comparison of circuit families.
6. Explain the Transmission gate and the tristate inverter briefly.
7. Describe with neat diagrams the Multiplexer and latches using transmission Gate.
8. Elaborate the concept of Delay estimation, logical effort and sizing of MOSFET.

CHAPTER 3

SEQUENTIAL LOGIC CIRCUITS

In sequential circuits, the output depends not only on the current values of the circuit inputs, but also on preceding input values.

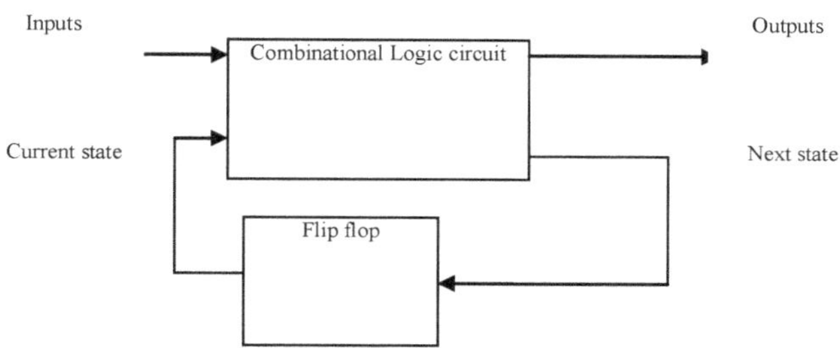

Figure 3.1: Block Diagram of a FSM Using Memory

Synchronous sequential system: If all storage registers are under control of a single global clock, then it is called synchronous sequential system. Registers may be positive edge triggered or negative edge triggered. Memory is organized as individual registers or register banks.

3.1. Classification of Memory Elements

Memories can be classified as static or dynamic. Static memories preserve the state as long as the power is ON. Static memories are constructed by positive feedback from output to of combinational circuit. It configures data loaded at the time of power-on. Multivibrator circuits are good example for positive feedback. Bistable Multivibrator is the most popular representation. Dynamic memories store data for a short period of time. They are based on the principle of charge stored on parasitic capacitors associated with MOS devices. The capacitors have to be refreshed periodically to compensate for charge leakage. Dynamic memories results in significant high performance and low power dissipation.

3.2. Static Latch

A latch is used for the construction of an edge-triggered register. It is a level sensitive circuit that passes the D input to the Q output when the clock signal is high. This latch is said to be in transparent node. When the clock is low, the latch is in hold mode. According to this type of principle it is called positive latch. A negative latch passes the D input to the Q output when the clock sign is low.

Latches are cascaded to construct registers. Level sensitive latches only sample the input on a clock transition 0 → 1 is called positive edge triggered and 1 → is called negative edge triggered.

If the register, sample the input on 0 → 1 clock transition, it is called positive edge triggered register of the register sample the input on 1 → 0 clock transition, it is called negative edge triggered register.

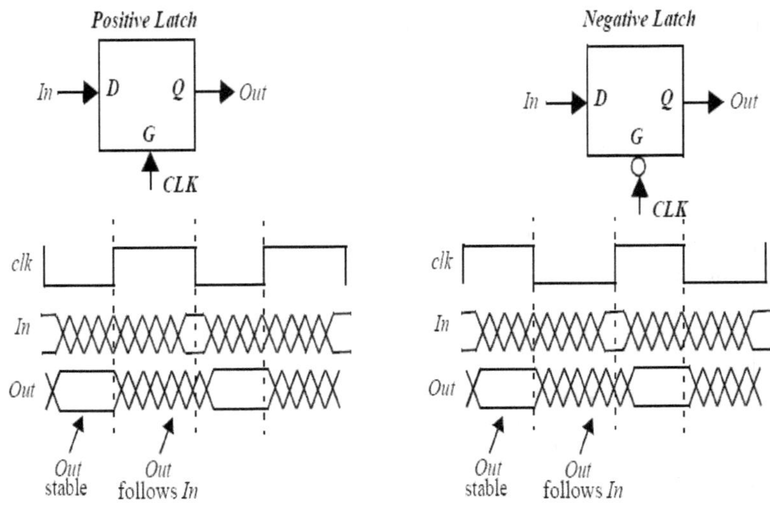

Figure 3.2: Positive and Negative Latch

Static memories use positive feedback to 'store two stable states 'o' and '1'. Basic concept is explained below. The two inverters are connected in cascade and its voltage transfer characteristics are given.

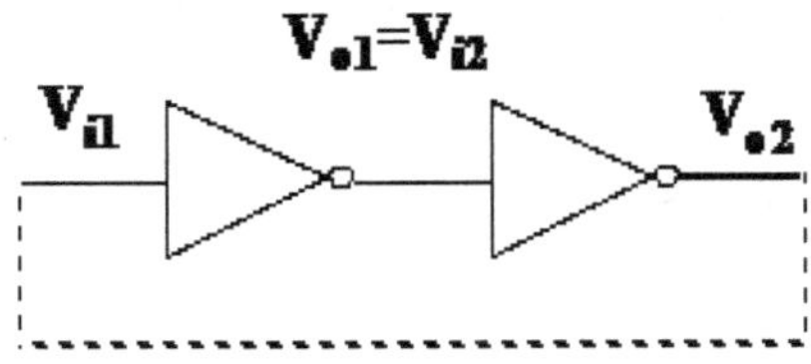

Figure 3.3: Two Cascaded Inverters

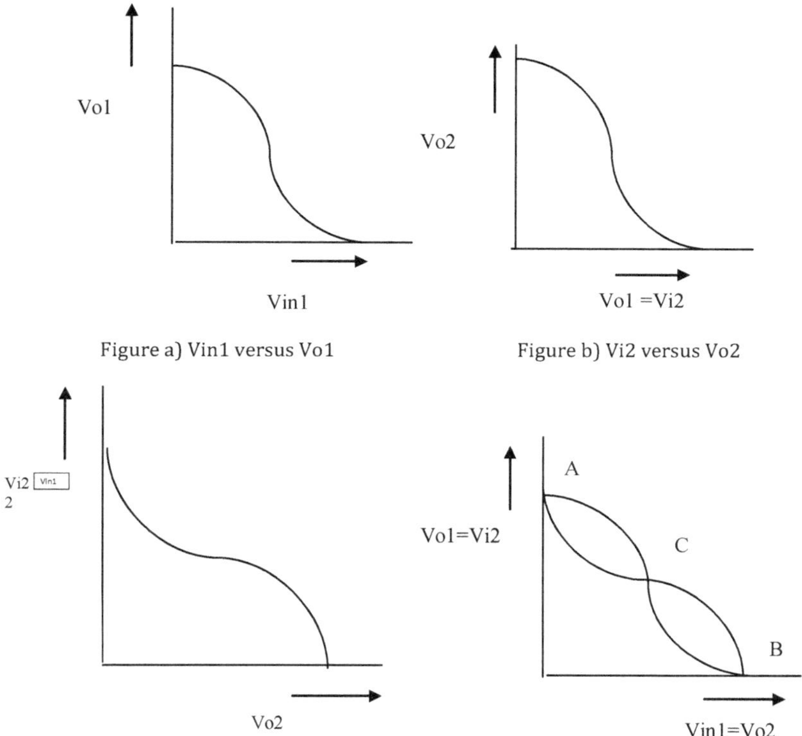

Figure a) Vin1 versus Vo1   Figure b) Vi2 versus Vo2

Figure c) Rotation of Fig b   Figure d) Resulting Circuit by Combining Figure a & Fig.c

Figure 3.4: Voltage Transfer Characteristics

The resulting circuit has three operating points A, B and C. A and B are the stable operating points and C is a metastable operating point. Suppose cross coupled inverter pair is biased at point C, a small deviation from the point causes noise which is amplified and regenerated around the closed loop. At the result the gain becomes more than unity. It results in oscillation. At the points A and B, the loop gain is smaller than unity. The cross coupling of two inverters results in a bistable circuit.

A bistable circuit has two stable states, the circuit remains in one state in the absence remains in one state in the absence of triggering. Another common name for bistable circuit is a flip flop.

3.2.1. *Multiplexer based Latches*

Positive and negative static latches based on multiplexer are shown below. For a negative latch, when the clock is low input o of the multiplexer ie D is selected and passed to the output. When clock is high, input 1 of the mux which is connected to output is selected.

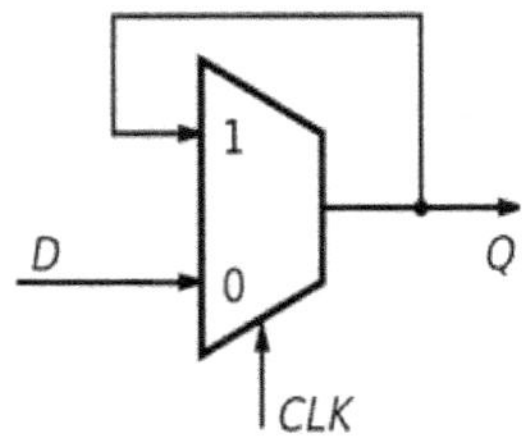

Figure 3.5: Negative Latch Using MUX

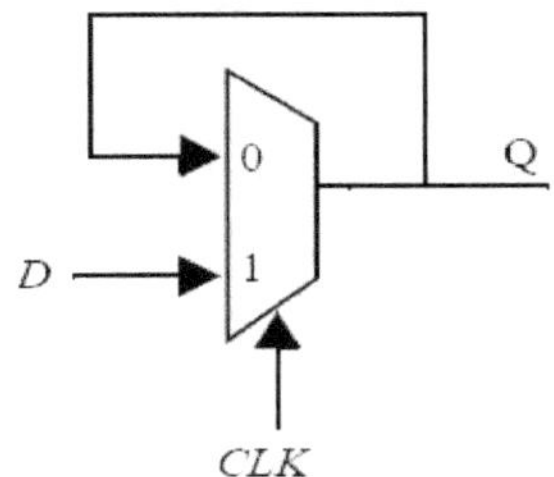

Figure 3.6: Positive Latch Using MUX

TG based positive latch based on MUX is shown below. When clk equal to high, the bottom transmission gate is on and the latch is transparent ie D input is copied to the Q. During this time the feedback loop is open. The number of transistors that clock drives is an important metric for calculation of power dissipation. The above structure presents a load of 4 transistors to the clk.

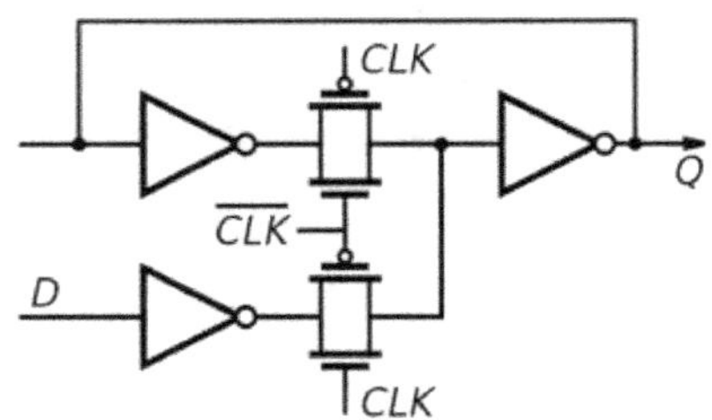

Figure 3.7: Positive Latch Using Transmission Gate

3.2.2. NMOS Pass Transistor based Latch

Another structure is given which uses NMOS pass transistors to reduce the load of 2 transistors to the clk. When clk is high, the latch process the D input and the circuit go to hold state when clk is low.

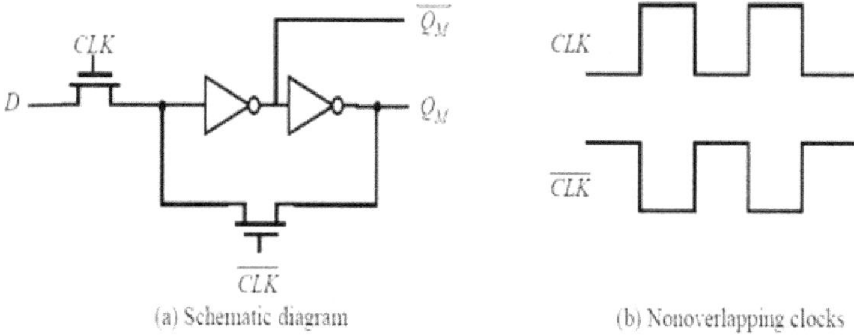

Figure 3.8: NMOS Pass Transistor based Latch

3.2.3. Master-Slave Edge Triggered Register

The register consists of cascading a negative latch (Master stage) with a positive one (slave stage). When clock is low, the master is transparent and D input is passed to the master stage output. In this stage slave is in hold mode. When clock is high the slave stage process the master output, while the master stage remains in the hold stage.

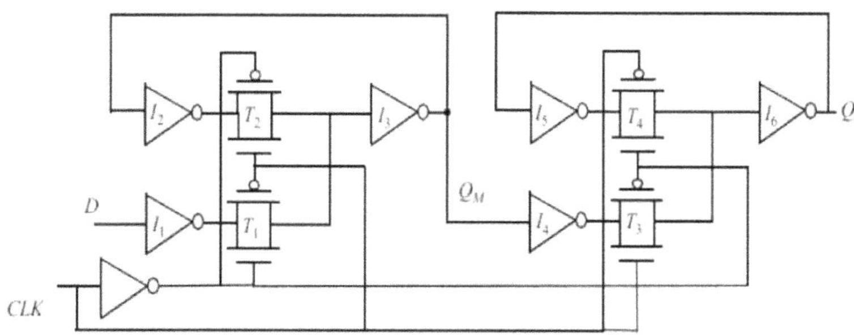

Figure 3.9: Master-Slave Edge Triggered Register

3.2.4. Static SR Latch

The NOR latch is shown in Fig. The second input to NOR gate is connected to the trigger inputs (S and R) that make it possible to force the outputs Q and $\overline{Q}$ to a given state.

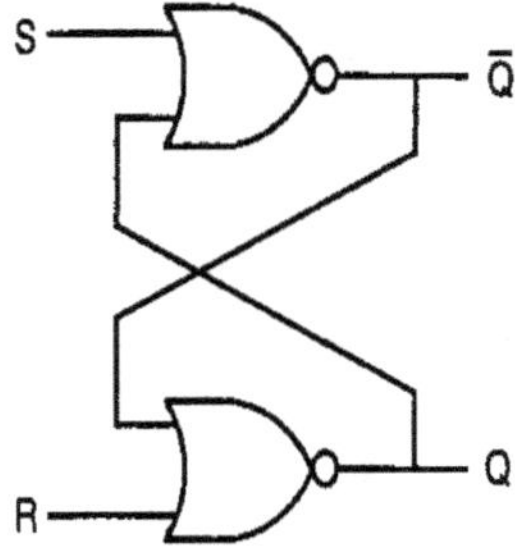

Figure 3.10: Diagram of SR Latch

Table 3.1: Characteristic Table

S	R	Q	$\overline{\overline{Q}}$
0	0	Q	$\overline{Q}$
1	0	1	0
0	1	0	0
1	1	Indeterminate	

When both S and R are 0, the flip flop's both outputs retain their state. If both inputs are 1, the output values are in indeterminate state. A '1' input applied to S input makes the Q output forced to '1'. A pulse on 'R' resets the flip flop and Q output goes to 'o'. The characteristic table explains the operation of SR Flip flop.

3.2.5. SR FF using NAND Gate

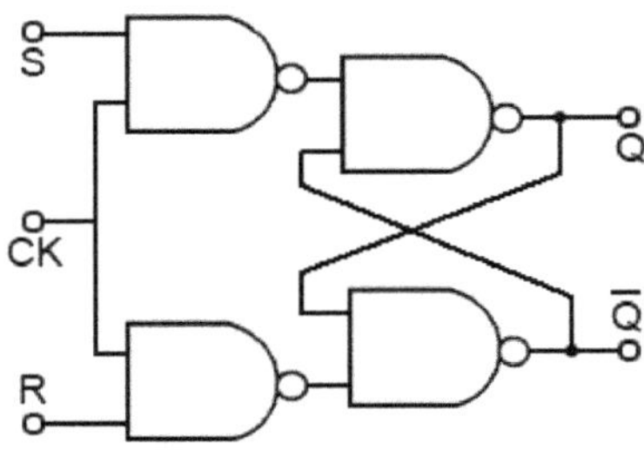

Figure 3.11: SR FF Using NAND Gate

A clocked version of the Latch is shown in above Fig. It consists of cross coupled inverter plus four extra transistors to drive the flip- flop from one state to another. In steady state, the inverter resides in steady state.

3.3. Dynamic Latches and Registers

The major disadvantage of a static gate is its complexity. The stored value remains valid as long as supply voltage is applied to the circuit. The registers used in structures based on temporary storage of charge on parasitic capacitors are called dynamic registers.

Capacitance storage principle is used in dynamic latch. Charge stored on a capacitance can be used to represent a logic signal. The absence of charge denotes 0, which the presence of charge denotes 1. Due to sub threshold leakage problem, the charge stored on dynamic nodes are discharged. So dynamic nodes retain their values only for short period of time, typically in the range of milliseconds.

3.3.1. *Dynamic Transmission Gate -based Edge Trigged Register*

Dynamic positive edge-Triggered register based on the master-slave concept is shown below. When clk = 0, input data is sampled on node A which has equivalent capacitance C_1. The slave stage is in hold state. On the rising edge of the CLK, T_2 turns on and the value in A is propagated to output Q. Node 2 stores the inverse of node 1. Edge triggered register is very efficient because it uses eight transistors.

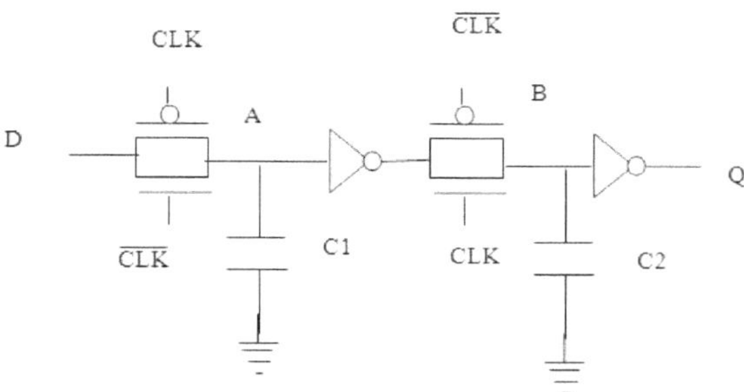

Figure 3.12: Transmission Gate-based Edge Trigged Register

3.3.2. *Clocked CMOS Register (C² MOS Register)*

It is constructed by cascading master stage with slave.

- When CLK equal to 0, the master stage acts as an inverter sampling the inverted D. Master is in Evaluation and slave is in high impedance state. Both transistors M_7 and M_8 are off isolating the output from input. The output Q retains its previous value stored in CL_2.

- When CLK equal to 1, the master is in hold state, second stage is in evaluation M_7 and M_8 transistors are ON. The value stored on CL_1 propagates to the output node through the slave stage.

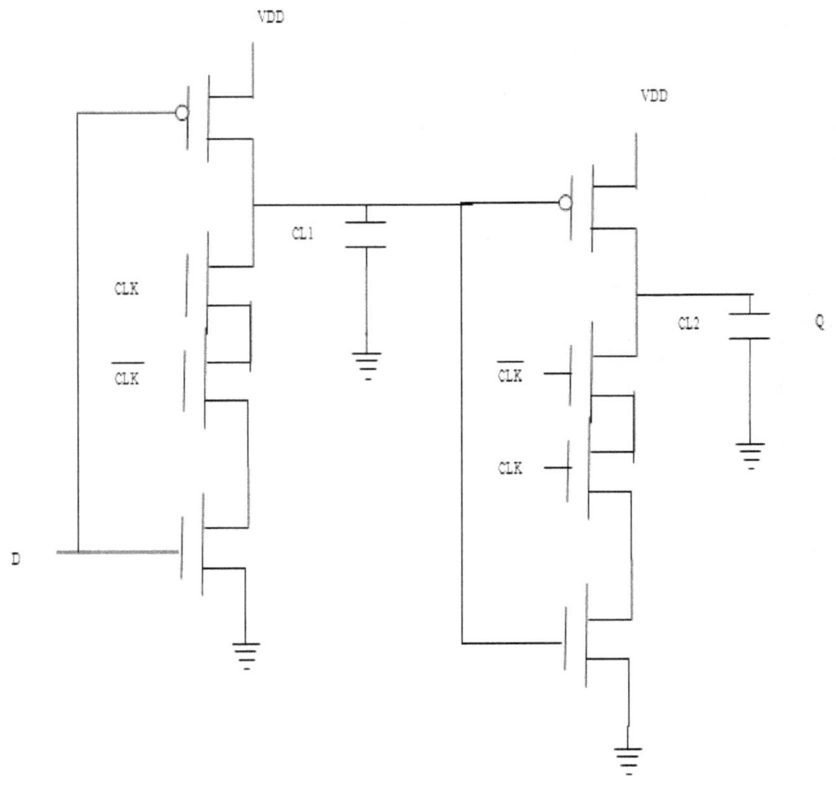

Figure 3.13: Clocked CMOS Register

3.3.3. *True Single-Phase Clocked Register (TSPCR)*

The single phase positive latch is shown below. When the CLK is high, the latch is in transparent node and two inverters coming into cascade. So the latch is non inverting and propagates input to output.

When CLK equal to 0, both inverters are disabled and the latch is in a hold mode. So no signal can propagate from input of the latch to the output.

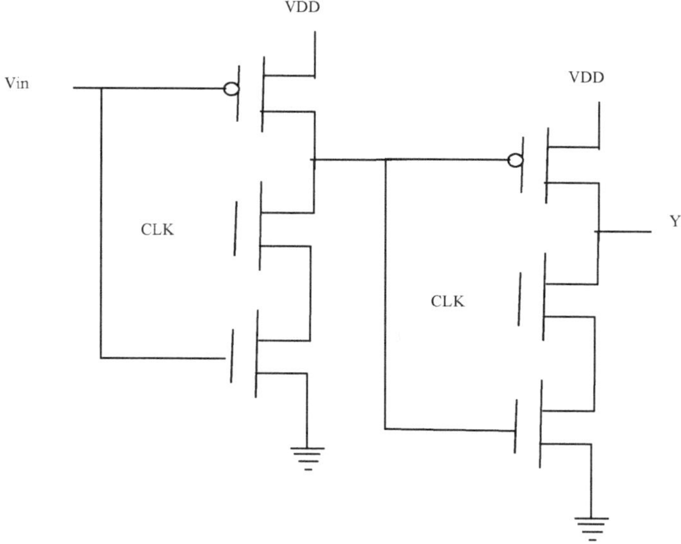

Figure 3.14: Positive Single Phase Latch

Register can be constructed by cascading positive and negative latch. The advantage is the use of single clock phase. Disadvantage is number of transistors are increased. Implementation of register requires 12 transistors.

Simple NMOS pass transistor and transmission can act as dynamic latch. $\overline{CLK}$ can be generated from additional generator or by inverting CLK. By adding inverter in the output of transistor inverting latch can be formed.

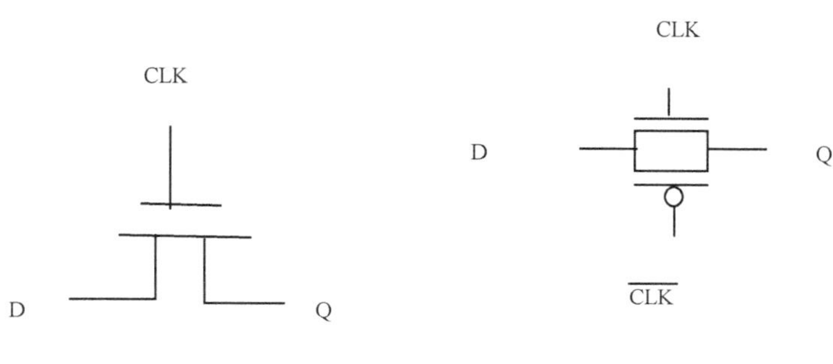

a) Latch Using NMOS Pass Transistor   b) Latch Using TG

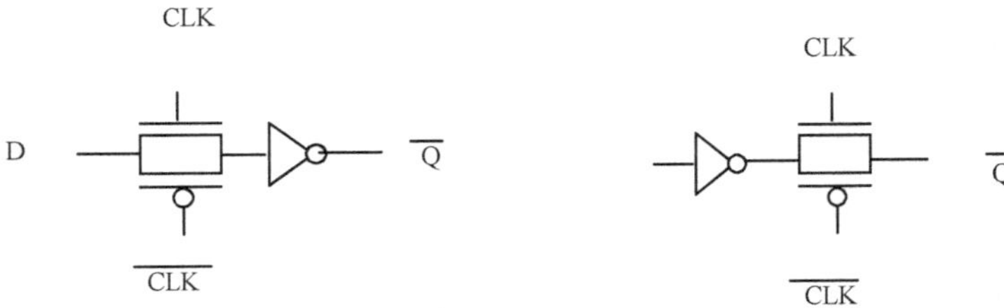

c) Buffered Output Inverting Latch   d) Buffered Input Inverting Latch

Figure 3.15: Implementation of Latch

3.4. Pipelining

It is an approach to optimize sequential circuits. It is a popular design technique used to accelerate the operation of data paths in processors.

Simple example circuit for computation of log (a_1+b_1) is shown. Inputs a and b are the streams of numbers. Assume that Registers are edge triggered D registers.

$$T_{min} = t_{pq} + t_{pd} + t_{su}$$

Where tpd = Propagation delay through combinational circuits

t_{su} = setup time and   tpr = propagation delay of register.

If the delay of the register is ignored then such logic module is active for only one third of the clock period. Pipelining is to improve the resource utilization and increase functional throughput. If the registers are introduced between the logic blocks, the computation of one set of input data spreads over a number of clock periods.

Clock period	Adder	Absolute value	Logarithm
1	$a_1 + b_1$		
2	a_2+b_2	$|a_1+b_1|$	
3	a_3+b_3	$|a_2+b_2|$	$\log |a_1+b_1|$

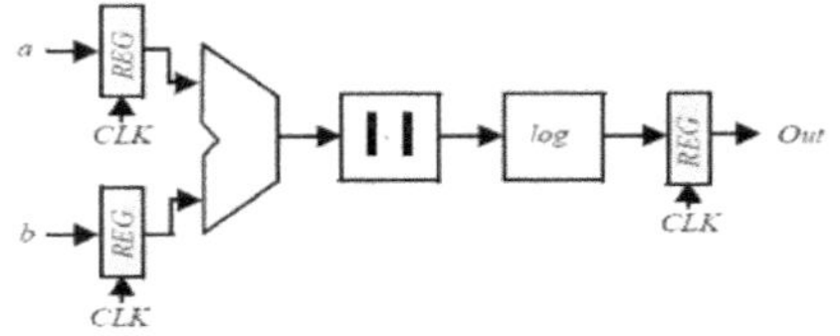

Figure 3.16: Pipelining Architecture

The result of (a_1, b_1) only appears to the output after three clock periods. At that time the circuit has performed part of the computation for next data sets.

The computational block has been partitioned into three sections.

Tmin.pip= t_{pq} + max (t_{pd}.add, t_{pd}.abs, t_{pd}.log)+t_{su}

Tmin.pip = Tmin/3 if suppose all three blocks of combinational circuit has same delay.

3.4.1. Pipelines Using Level-Sensitive Latches

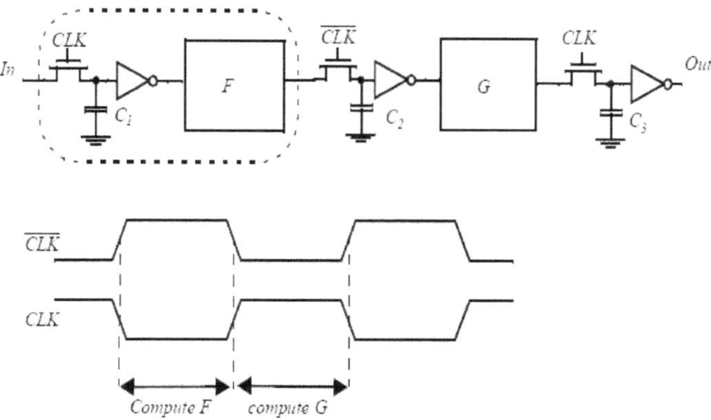

Figure 3.17: Two Phase Pipelined Circuit Using Dynamic Register

Pipeline system is implemented using pass transistor based positive and negative latches. Pipeline used between master- slave system is shown above. Input data is sampled at negative edge of the clock.

The result of the logic block F is stored on C_2 at -ve edge of the $\overline{CLK}$. At the same time the computation of G starts. The value stored on C_2 is the previous input passing through F. The race condition occurs when CLK and $\overline{CLK}$ overlaps.

3.4.2. Pipelining Using C²MOS Latches

C²MOS based pipelined circuit is race free as long as all the logic function F between latches are non inverting. F can be replaced by inverter. Another implementation that combines C²MOS pipeline registers and NOR dynamic logic function is shown below. It is called NORA-CMOS. Each module consists of black of combinational logic that can be a mixture of static and dynamic logic followed by C²MOS.

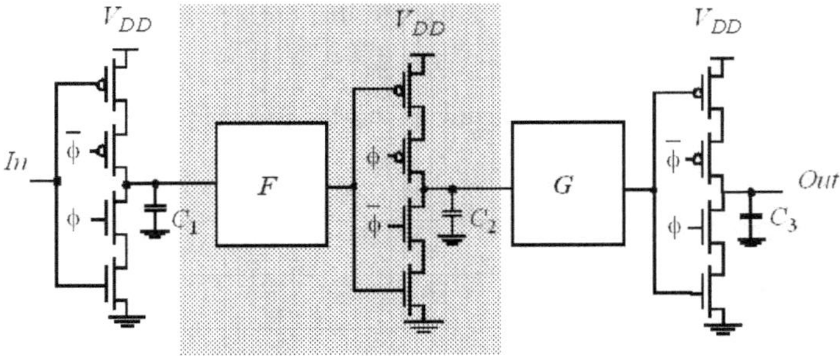

Figure 3.18: Pipelining Using C²MOS Latch

3.5.   Memory

The different types of memories are available. The memory is selected based on the size and access time. The memory size is represented in bytes or kilobytes, megabytes and Gigabytes. The time it takes to read from the memory is called read-access time, which is equivalent to difference between data available and request time.

Classification of Semiconductor Memories

1.   ROM: It belongs to nonvolatile memories ie disconnection of the supply voltage does not result in a loss of the stored data.

2.   NVRWM (Non volatile read write memory): EPROM (Erasable programmable Read only), E²PROM (Electrically Erasable programmable Read only) and flash memory comes into this category.

3.   RWM (Read write memory):

It is a most flexible memory because the data can be both read and write into this memory. Data are stored either in flip flops or as a charge on a capacitor. Based on the above principle the memory cells called static (SRAM) and dynamic (DRAM) respectively. It is a volatile memory because the data is lost when power supply is turned OFF.

Memory Architecture

Architectural of N word * M bits memory is shown below. The size of the bits stored in each word is M bits. This approach works well for smaller memories and leads to a problem when implementing larger memories. The main problem is access time is large and speed is low. The vertical wires connecting storage cells to the I/O becomes excessively long. So automatically the delay of the interconnect increases as its length increases.

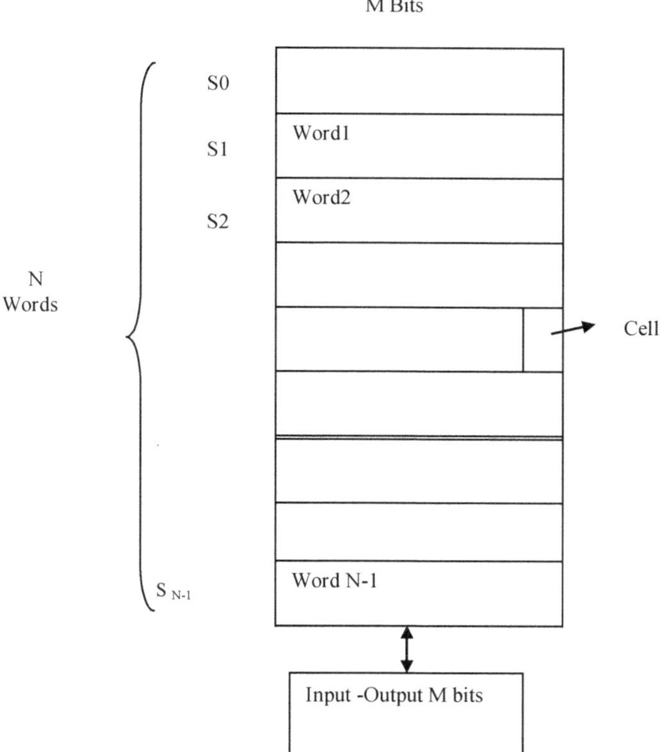

Figure 3.19: Architecture of N*M Array Memory

Each storage cell is a DFF and select signal is used to activate the cell. Any one of the select signal S can be high to activate the cell. For $N=10^6$ and $M=8$ (1 Mega word memory) 1 million select lines are needed. This is the major drawback.

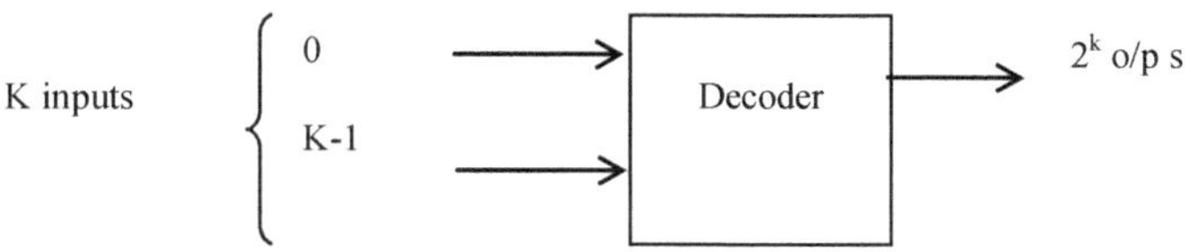

Figure 3.20: Block Diagram of Decoder

Decoder reduces the number of select signals. The decoder translates the address into $N=2^k$ select lines, only one of which is active at a line. It reduces the number of address lines.

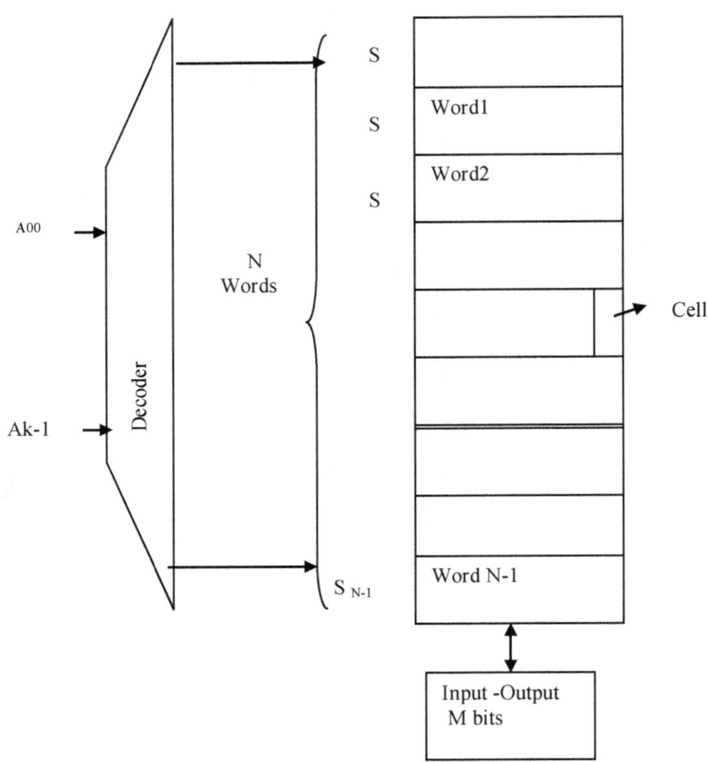

Figure 3.21: Architecture of Memory Using Decoder

3.5.1. *Array-Structured Memory Organization*

Memory arrays are organized so that vertical and horizontal dimensions are of same order of magnitude. Multiple words are stored in a single row and are selected simultaneously; column decoder is used to route correct word to the input/output terminals.

The address word is partitioned into a column address (A_0- A_{k-1}) and a row address (A_0 to A_{L-1}). Reducing the size of the basic memory storage cell saves memory area.

This architecture works well for memories up to a range of 64k bits to 256 k bits. Larger memories suffer speed degradation due to capacitance and resistance effect.

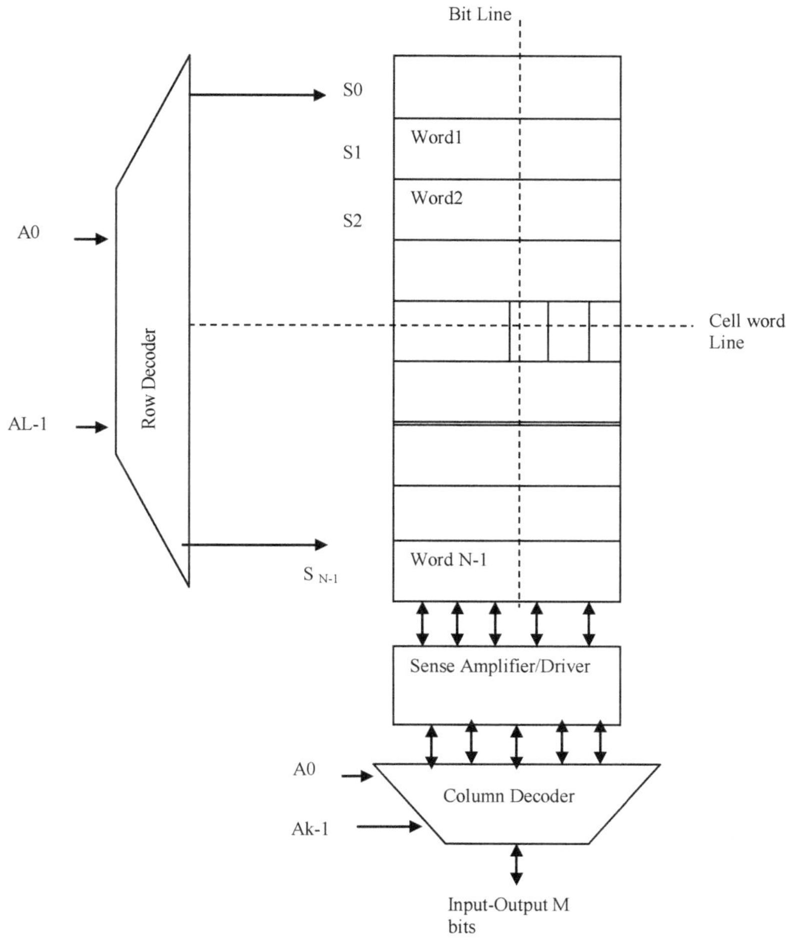

Figure 3.22: Array Structured Memory Organization

3.5.2. *Hierarchical Memory Architecture*

The memory is partitioned in to smaller blocks. Each block is in Array-structure. A word is selected on the basis of row and column addresses. Block addresses select one of the p blocks to be read or write. The block address activates only one of the address blocks at a time. Non active blocks are put in power saving mode. This reduces power dissipation. Access time is very less and memory is fast

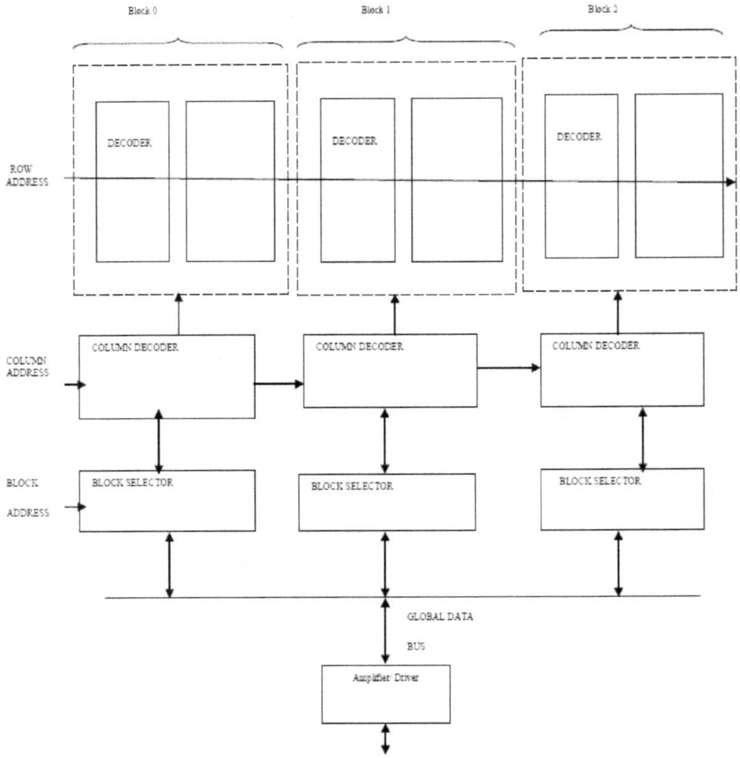

Figure 3.23: Array Structured Memory Organization

3.5.3. *Content - Addressable Memory Architecture*

The following Figure shows an example of 512 word CAM memory which supports three modes of operation: read, write and match. The compared block is filled with data pattern to match. To find all words in the CAM array that have the pattern OX123 in MSB, compare block has to be filled with OX12300000 and the mask with OXFFF00000. Mask word indicates which bit is significant. All 512 rows of CAM array simultaneously compare 12 most significant bits of compare with data obtained in the row. Every row that matches the pattern is passed on to validity block. If many row sends the data with same pattern, priority encoder selects one with highest address and encode it.

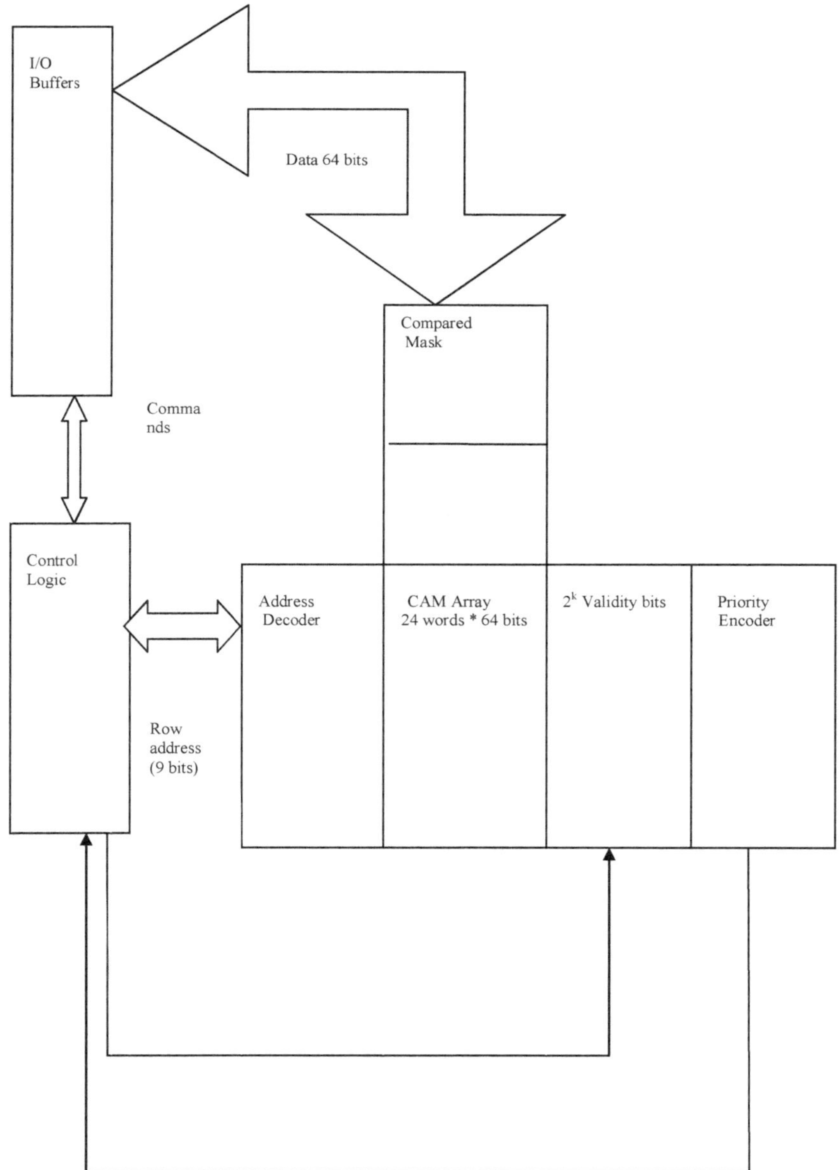

Figure 3.24: Architecture of 512 Word-Content Addressable Memory

3.6. ROM Memory

ROM memory contents can only be read. It is used in applications such as washing machines, calculators, and games need only reading for storing the Programs.

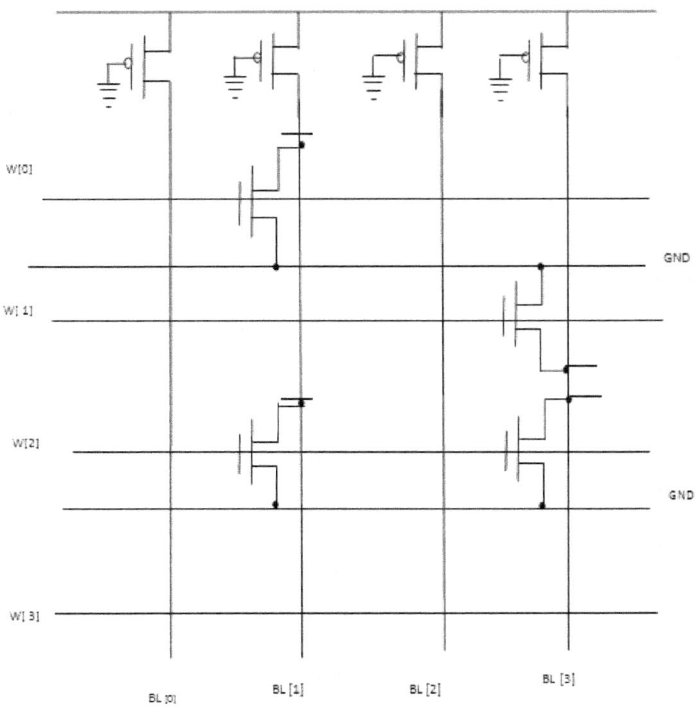

Figure 3.25: 4*4 ROM Array

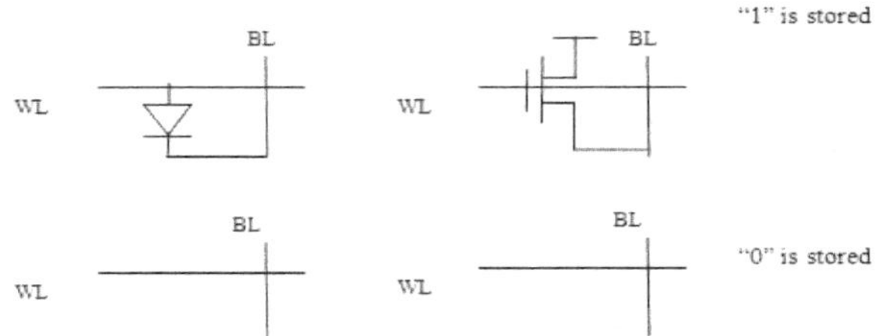

Figure 3.26: Different Approaches for Implementing 1 and 0 in ROM Cells

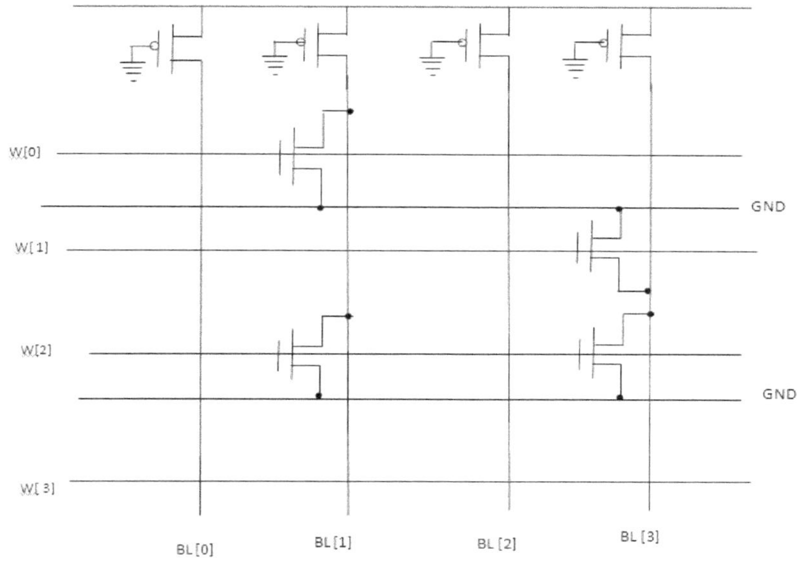

Figure 3.27: 4*4 NOR ROM Array

The simplest cell is a diode-based ROM cell is shown in Figure 3.26. The BL is pulled low through a resistor connected to ground. Since no physical connection between BL and WL, the value of BL is low. When a voltage is applied to WL, the diode is enabled and word line is pulled up resulting in a 1 on the bit line. It consumes large current. So it is not suitable for large memories. Instead of diode NMOS transistor is used for the cell. The drain of NMOS is connected to supply. All output driving current is provided by MOS transistor. An alternative implementation is to connect bit line to the supply. The default value at the output must equal 1. The absence of transistor between WL and BL means '1' is stored. The "0" is stored by connecting MOS device between bit line and ground.

3.7.   Non Volatile Read-Write Memories

It consists of an array of transistors placed on a word-line/bit line. The memory is programmed by selectively disabling or enabling some of those devices. In a ROM it is done as mask-level. The programmed values must be erased, after which a new programming round starts. The method of erasing differs for each and every technique. Floating gate transistor is the heart of most reprogrammable memories. The threshold voltage of this transistor is programmable.

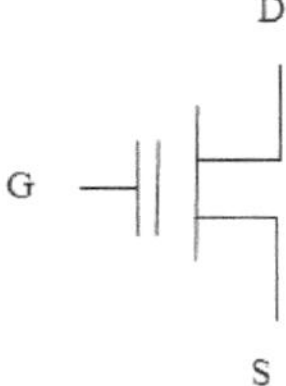

Figure 3.28: Schematic Symbol of Floating Gate MOS

3.8.   EPROM

Content in the EPROM is erased by passing ultraviolet rays on the cells through a transparent window. The erasure process is slow and it takes from seconds to several minutes. Programming takes microseconds per word. The device threshold also varies with repeated programming cycles. Most EPROM memories contain on-chip circuit to control the value of the thresholds. Using EPROM large memories at low cost can be fabricated.

3.9.   EEPROM or E^{2}PROM

The erasure procedure in EPROM should occur "OFF system" ie the memory must be removed from the board and placed EPROM programmer for programming EEPROM avoids those by using tunneling mechanism to inject or remove charge from the A modified floating gate device called FLOTOX (Floating gate tunneling oxide) transistor is used as programmable device.

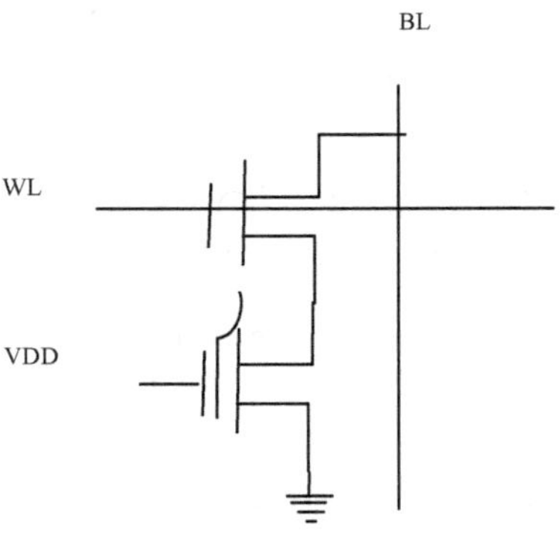

Figure 3.29: EEPROM Cell Configured During Read Operation

3.10. Flash Electrically Erasable Programmable ROM

It is a combination of EPROM and EPROM. It uses the avalanche hot-election injection approach to program the devices. Erasure is performed using Fowler-Nordhein tunneling. It is called flash memory.

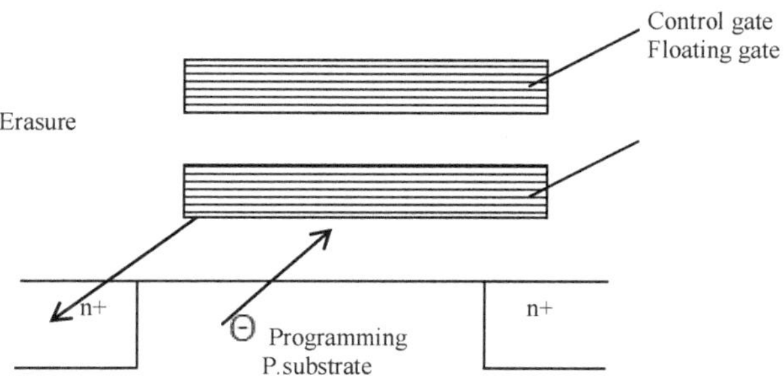

Figure 3.30: ETOX Device Used in Flash EEPROM

3.11. Read Write Memory

This type of memory can be read and write. This is also called RAM.

3.11.1. Static Random Access Memory (SRAM)

SRAM using six transistors is shown in Fig. Two bit lines are required .Pass transistors M_5 and M_6 are shared between read and write operation.

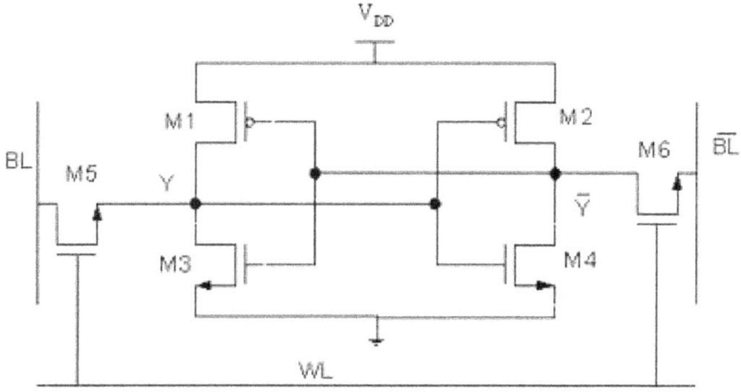

Figure 3.31: Six Transistors SRAM Cell

Read and Write Operation

Assume that a 1 is stored at Q and also bit lines are precharged to 2.5 V .The read cycle is started by asserting WL Bit storage is obtained using bit stability property of the cross coupled inverter M_5 and M_6 are called Access transistors and are used to provide conduction paths to the internal bit storage. The access FETs are controlled by the word line signal WL. When WL=0 both transistors are OFF and the cell is in a hold state. To perform read or write operation the word line is get to WL=1. A read occurs when the internal states are transmitted out of the cell via the access transistors. To write a data bit d to the cell, d is placed in BL and $\overline{d}$ is placed in $\overline{BL}$. Assume for a write operation a 1 is stored in the cell (ie Q=1). A '0' is written in the cell by setting $\overline{BL}$ to 1 and BL=0.

3.11.2. Dynamic RAM

DRAMS have the lowest cost per bit because they are simple. The basic 1 transistor DRAM cell is shown in Fig. It consists of NMOS M1 and storage capacitor C_s. The top of capacitor is connected to access transistor, while the bottom line is grounded. To write a bit, the word line is elevated to a logic, voltage, WL = 1 turns on the M_1. The data voltage is applied to bit line. The charge stored on C_s is given by $Qs=C_sVs$ so that logic" 0" and logic"1" values are differentiated by small and large charge level.

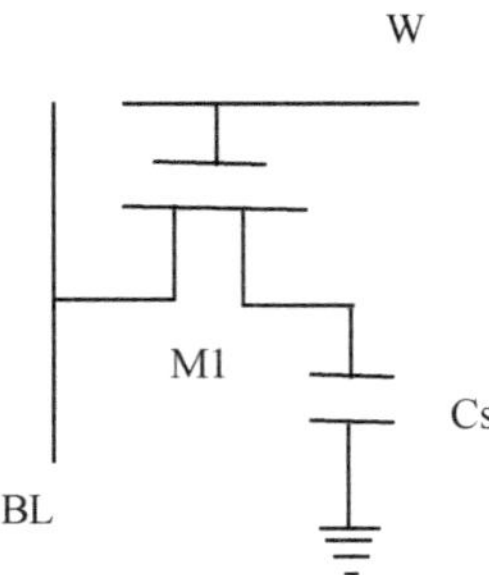

Figure 3.32: One Transistor Dynamic RAM Cell

A hold condition is attained by bringing WL=0. This makes M, into cutoff and blocks the main conduction path to the bit line. When DRAM cell is in hold state, the leakage currents through the transistor reduce the amount of charge stored. This has no effect on logic o, but destroys logic 1 charge level. Sub threshold conduction is the most important reason for leakage current. Frequent refresh operation is needed. The content of the cell are read, amplified and rewritten.

$$I_{leak} = Cs\,\frac{\Delta vs}{\Delta t}$$

$$\Delta vs = \frac{Ileak}{Cs}\,\Delta t$$

Δt = Time interval that the charge has been held.

$$\frac{t_h}{(hold\,Time)} = \frac{Cs}{I_{leak}}[Vs(o)-v_1]$$

Vs (0) = Initial voltage on capacitor.

V_1= Minimum voltage that can be recognized as logic.

Address Decoder

Row decoder and column decoders are used to select a particular cell in a memory array.

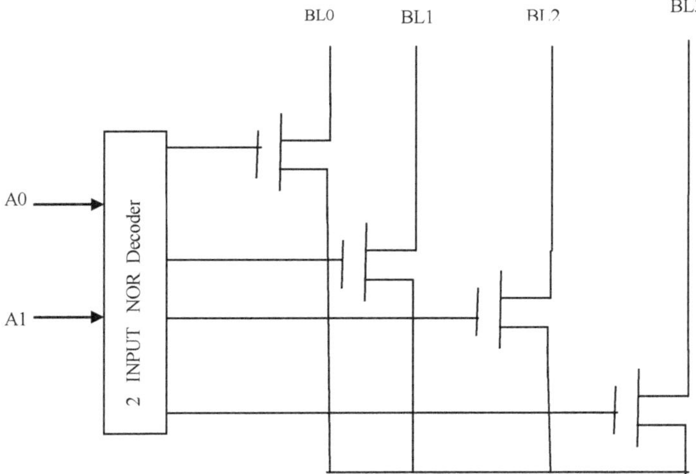

Figure 3.33: Four Input Pass Transistor-based Column Decoder using a NOR Decoder

The control signal of the pass transistors are generated using K - 2^k pre-decoder realized by NOR. The main advantage of this decoder is its speed because a single pass transistor is in the signal path and it introduces only small resistance. NOR decoders are faster but they consume more area than NAND decoder.

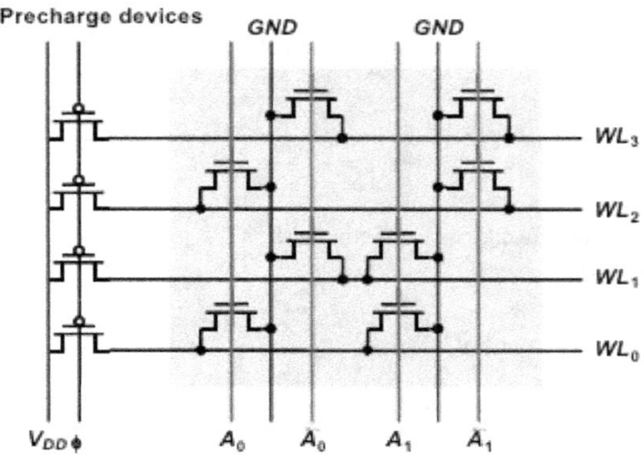

Figure 3.34: Dynamic 2 to 4 NOR Decoder

For Word Line Decoder

$$WL0 = \overline{Ao + A1} = \overline{Ao}.\overline{A1}$$

$$WL_1 = \overline{\overline{Ao} + A1} = Ao.\overline{A1}$$

$$WL_2 = \overline{Ao + \overline{A1}} = \overline{Ao}.A1$$

$$WL_3 = \overline{\overline{Ao} + \overline{A1}} = Ao.A1$$

Sense Amplifier

Sense Amplifiers perform the following function.

1. Amplification.
2. Delay reduction.
3. Power reduction.
4. Signal restoration.

Differential Voltage Sensing Amplifier

It is directly applicable to SRAM memories because they uses a true differential output current mirror concept. The amplifier is conditioned by the sense amplifier enable (SE) signal. M3 and M4 at as an active current mirror load. Inputs are fed to differential input devices (M1 and M2).

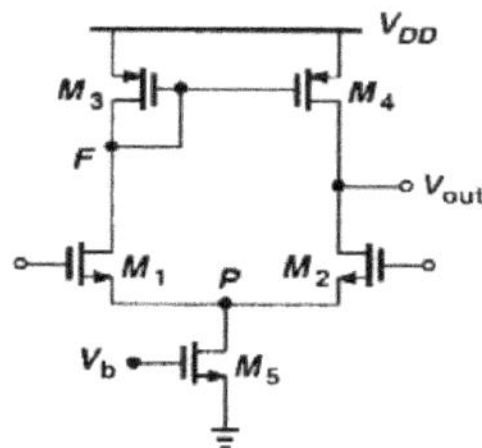

Figure 3.35: Differential Voltage Sensing Amplifier

3.12. Power Dissipation in Memories

Power dissipation in a memory chip is due to three sources: The memory cell array, decoder (row, column and block) and the peripherals used (sensors). The decoder charging current is also negligibly small and power dissipation due to sense amplifier is small because it is OFF when not in action. The main power dissipation is due to memory cell array.

Power dissipation is proportional to the size of the memory dividing the memory into sub arrays and keeping n and m small is essential to keep power within bounded value. The memory partitioning is accomplished by reducing m (the number of cells on a bite line). Memory units that are not in use should consume only power necessary for data retention. Partial activation of bit line in DRAM reduces the capacitance switched at every read / write operation.

3.13. Power Reduction in Memories

Reducing the voltage levels is one of the most efficient techniques to reduce power dissipation in memories. Data retention and reliability issues make challenge in the voltage scaling.

3.13.1. SRAM Active Power Reduction

The voltage swing on the bit line is made as small as possible typically between 0.1 v to 0.3v for fast read. Current flows in the bit line as long as word line is activated. Limiting Δt and bit line swing helps to keep the active dissipation of SRAMs low.

3.13.2. DRAM Active Power Reduction

The bit lines are charged and discharged over the full voltage swing (ΔVBL) for every read operation. The bit line dissipation charge should be reduced.

Bit line dissipation charge = $mC_{BL} \Delta VBL$ where m is the number of cells. If the bit line capacitance is reduced, power dissipation is reduced. Voltage reduction has to be accompanied by either an increase in the size of storage capacitor and or a noise reduction.

Data Retention Power Dissipation

Leakage current of the cell transistors is the major source of retention current.

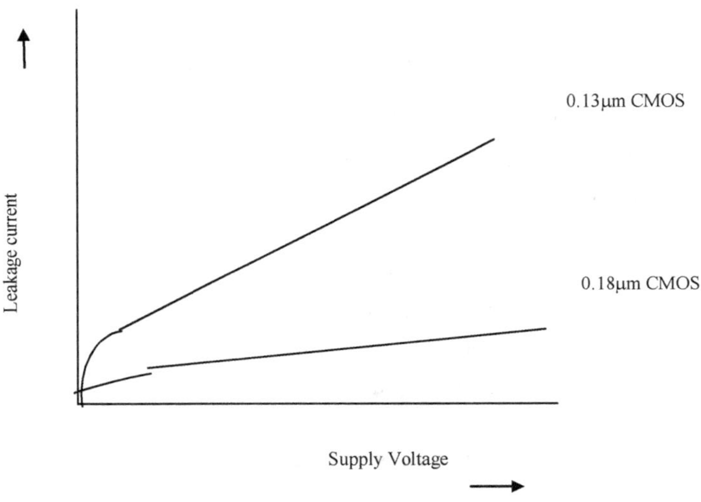

Figure 3.36: Leakage Current in 8k bit SRAM

From the above Figure it is understood that the same 8k bit SRAM implemented by using 0.13 µm CMOS consumes 7 times more current than implemented by using 0.18µm process. Methods to reduce retention current of SRAM memories are:

1. Turning off unused memory blocks.
2. Increasing the threshold his.
3. Inserting extra resistance in the leakage paths.
4. Lowering the supply voltage.

DRAM Retention Power Dissipation Reduction

The standby power is proportional to the bit line charge and refreshes frequency. One method to minimize leakage current is to control v_t. Standby leakage suppression techniques are shown in following Figure.

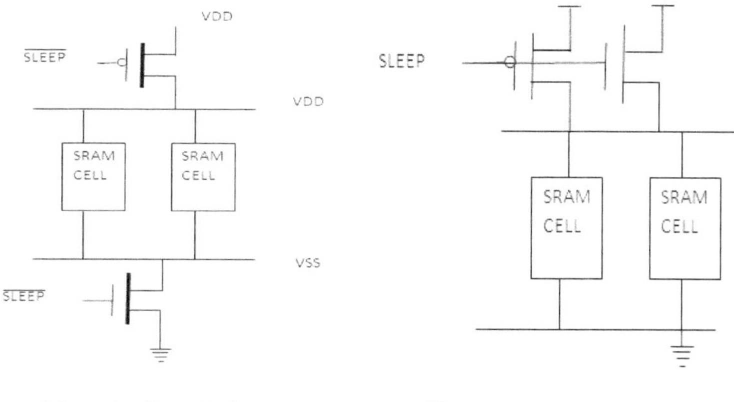

a) Inserting Extra Resistance   b) Lowering Supply Voltage

Figure 3.37: Standby Leakage Suppression Technique

3.14. Synchronizer

A synchronizer is a circuit that accepts an input that can change at arbitrary times and produces an output aligned to the synchronizer clock. .A synchronizer accepts are D and a clock, it produces an output Q that ought to be valid some delay after the clock.

Synchronizer Built from a Pair of FFs

This is the most simple and most common synchronization scheme and consists of two or more flip-flops in chain working on the destination clock domain. This approach allows for an entire clock period for the first flip flop to resolve metastability.

Handshaking based Synchronizer

Synchronization in Multibit data transfer is implemented by using handshaking signal where the transfer of data is controlled by handshaking protocol. The source domain places data on the 'REQ' signal. When it goes high, receiver knows data is stable on bus and it is safe to sample the data. After sampling, the receiver asserts 'ACK' signal. This signal is synchronized to the source domain and informs the sender that data has been sampled successfully and it may send a new data. Handshaking based synchronizers offer a good reliable communication but reduce data transmission bandwidth as it takes many cycles to exchange handshaking signals. Handshaking allows digital circuits to effectively communicate with each other when response time of one or both circuits is unpredictable.

Mux based Synchronizer

Two flip flop synchronizers are hazardous if used to synchronize data which is more than 1-bit in width. In such situations, we may use mux-based synchronization scheme. In this, the source domain sends an **enable** signal indicating that it the data has been changed. This **enable** is synchronized to the destination domain using the two flip flop synchronizer. The synchronized signal acts as an **enable** signal indicating that the data on the data bus from source is stable and destination domain may latch the data.

3.15. Synchronous and Asynchronous System

Synchronous System

All memory elements in this system are simultaneously updated using a globally distributed periodic synchronization signal (i.e., a global clock signal)

Asynchronous System

No need for a globally distributed clock, but have asynchronous circuit overheads (handshaking logic, etc.).

3.16. Timing Issues

Rise Time

The time needed for Vout to rise from 0.1 VDD to 0.9 VDD is known as Rise time.

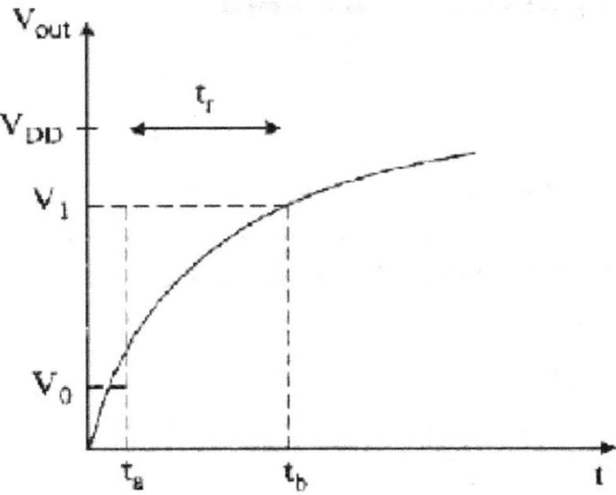

Figure 3.38: Rise Time

Fall Time

The time needed for Vout to fall from 0.9 VDD to 0.1 VDD is known as Fall time.

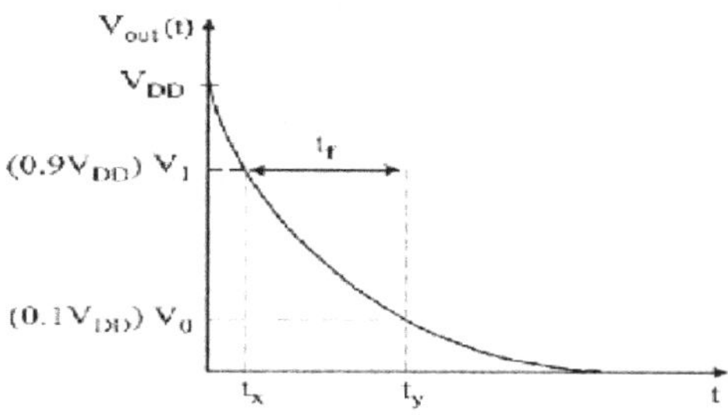

Figure 3.39: Fall Time

Maximum Signal Frequency

It is defined as the largest frequency (f) applied to gate and allows the output to settle to a definable state.

$$f = \frac{1}{tr + tf}$$

where, tr - Rise time

tf - fall time

f - maximum signal frequency

3.17. Clocking Strategies

Clock signal generation and distribution in a digital system is to minimize

1. Clocks skew (spatial variations in clock edges).
2. Clock jitter (temporal variations in clock edges).

The selection of appropriate clocking strategy is an important issue in chip design. The clocking scheme affects the functionally speed and power of a circuit.

The most robust method of clocking is the two phase master-slave design. Two clock phases are generated by simply inverting the clock. Clock skew and jitter limit the performance of a digital system, so designing a clock network that minimizes both is important. In many high-speed processors, a majority of the dynamic power is dissipated in the clock network.To reduce dynamic power, the clock network must support clock gating. Balanced paths (H-tree network, matched RC trees) in the ideal case, can eliminate skew.

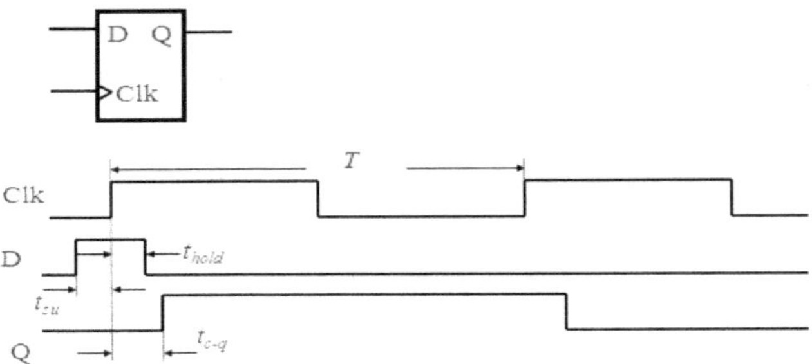

Figure 3.40: Diagram Showing Hold and Setup Time

Setup time (tsu) is the time period prior to the clock becoming active (edge or level) during which the flip-flop inputs must remain stable. It is shown in Figure 3.40.

Hold time (thold) is the time after the clock becomes inactive during which the flip-flop inputs must remain stable. It is shown in Figure 3.40.

Refer the Figure 3.41 for Min and Max delay constraint.

Min delay constraint: The path begins with the rising edge of the clock triggering FF1. The data may begin to change at Q1 after a clk-to-Q contamination delay. However, it must not reach D2 until at least the hold after the clock edge. Hence for minimum logic contamination delay

$$tcd >= thold - tccq$$

Max delay constraint: The path begins with the rising edge of the clock triggering FF1. The data must propagate to the output of the flip flop Q1 and through the combinational logic to D2, setting up at FF2 before the next rising clock edge. Under ideal conditions, the worst case propagation delays determine the minimum clock period for this sequential circuitry.

$$Tc >= tpcq + tpd + tsetup$$

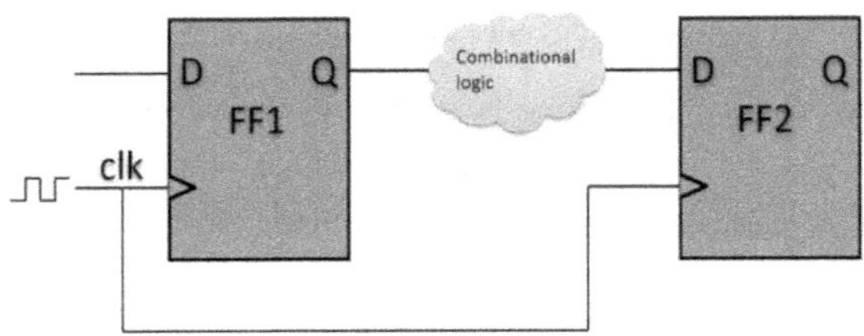

Figure 3.41: Flip–Flop Connection

2 Marks with Answer

1. What is called static and dynamic sequencing element?

A sequencing element with static storage employs some sort of feedback to retain its output value indefinitely. A sequencing element with dynamic storage generally maintains its value as charge on a capacitor that will leak away if not refreshed for a long period of time.

2. What is clock skew?

In reality clocks have some uncertainty in their arrival times that can cut into the time available for useful computation is called clock skew.

3. What are synchronizers?

Synchronizers are used to reduce metastability. The synchronizers ensure synchronization between asynchronous input and synchronous system.

4. What is the difference between mealy and moore state machines?

In the mealy state machine we can calculate the next state and output both from the input and state. But in the moore state machine we can calculate only next state but not output from the input and the state and the output is issued according to next state.

5. Define propagation delay and contamination delay?

Propagation delay(t pd): The amount of time needed for a change in a logic input to result in a permanent change at an output, that is the combinational logic will not show any further output changes in response to an input change alter time fod units

Contamination delay(tcd): The amount of time needed for a change in a logic input to result in an initial change at an output, that is the combinational logic is guaranteed not to show any output change in response to an input change before fed time units have passed.

6. Define Setup time and Hold time.

Setup time (t setup): The amount of time before the clock edge that data input D must be stable the rising clock edge arrives.

Hold time (t hold): This indicates the amount of time after the clock edge arrives the data input D must be held stable in order for FF to latch the correct value. Hold time is always measured from the rising clock edge to a point after the clock edge.

7. Difference between latches and Flip-Flop.

S.No	Latch	Flip-Flop
1.	A Latch is Level-Sensitive	A FF is edge triggered.
2.	A latch stores when the clock level is low and is transparent when the level is high.	A FF stores when the clock rises and is mostly never transparent.

8.   Define Pipelining.

Pipelining is a popular design technique often used to accelerate the operation of the data path in digital processors. The major advantages of pipelinig are to reduce glitching in complex logic networks and getting lower energy due to operand isolation.

9.   How the limitations of a ROM-based realization is overcome in a PLA-based realization.

In a ROM, the encoder part is only programmable and use of ROMs to realize Boolean functions is wasteful in many situations because there is no cross-connect for a significant part. This wastage can be overcome by using Programmable Logic Array (PLA), which requires much lesser chip area.

10. In what way the DRAMs differ from SRAMs?

Both SRAMs and DRAMs are volatile in nature, ie. Information is lost if power line is removed. However SRAMs provide high switching speed, good noise margin but require large chip area than DRAMs.

11. Explain the read and write operations for a one-transistor DRAM cell.

A significant improvement in the DRAM evolution was to realize 1-T DRAM cell. One additional capacitor is explicitly fabricated for storage purpose. To store 'I', it is charged to store '0' it is discharged to '0' volt. Read operation is destructive. Sense amplifier is needed for reading. Read operation is followed by restoration operation.

12. What do you meant by Max delay constraint and Min delay constraint?

Min delay constraint: the path begins with the rising edge of the clock triggering F1. The data may begin to change at Q1 after a clk-to-Q contamination delay. However, it must not reach D2 until at least the hold after the clock edge. Hence, we solve for minimum logic contamination delay:

$$tcd >= thold - tccq$$

Max delay constraint: the path begins with the rising edge of the clock triggering F1. The data must propagate to the output of the flip flop Q1 and through the combinational logic to D2, setting up at F2 before the next rising clock edge. Under ideal conditions, the worst case propagation delays determine the minimum clock period for this sequential circuitry

$$Tc >= tpcq + tpd + tsetup$$

13. Draw the schematic of 2:1 multiplexer using switch logic.

14. How to overcome the cascading problem of CMOS dynamic logic?

There are various solutions to the problem of how to cascade dynamic logic gates. One solution is Domino Logic, which inserts an ordinary static inverter between stages.

15. Draw the circuit diagram for SR latch using NOR gate Version

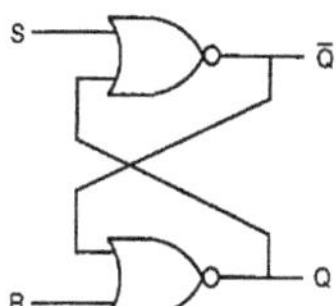

16. Draw the circuit diagram for SR latch using NAND gate.

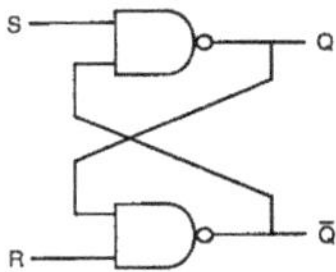

17. Draw the circuit diagram for clocked SR latch using NOR gate Version

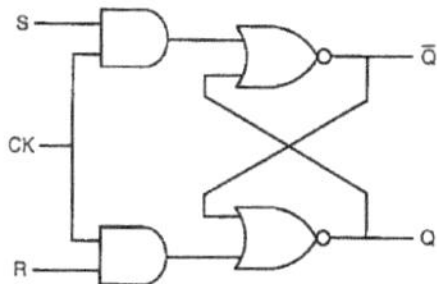

18. Draw the circuit diagram for clocked SR latch using NOR gate Version using CMOS

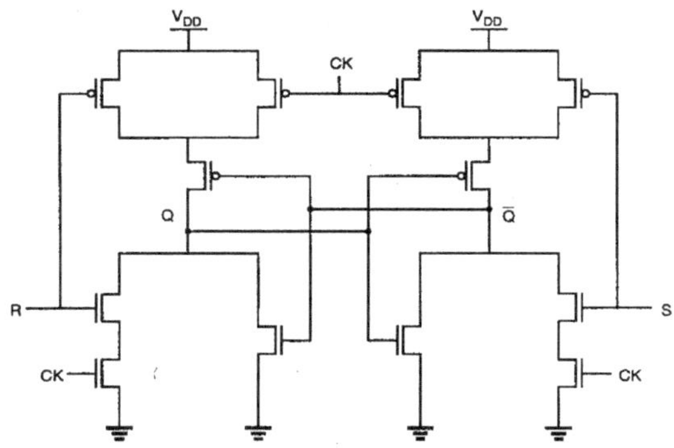

19. Draw the circuit for D Flip-flop

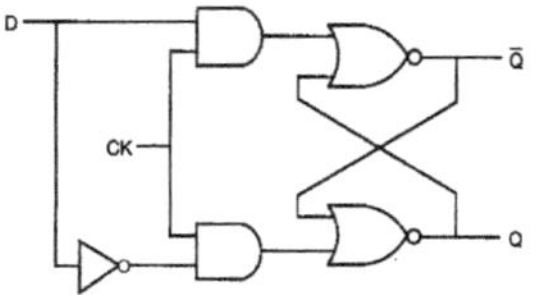

20. Draw the circuit for D latch using CMOS

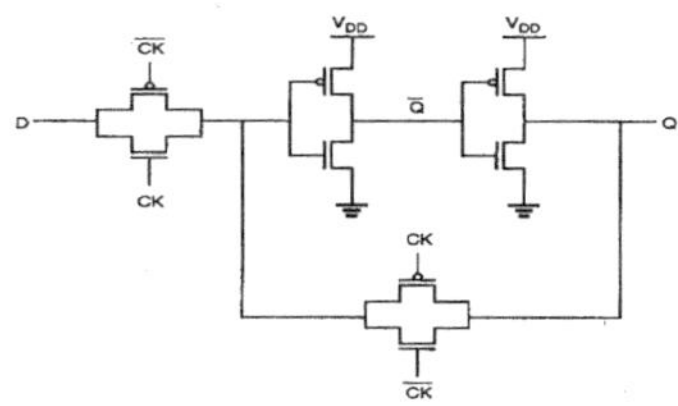

21. Different types of Memory Arrays

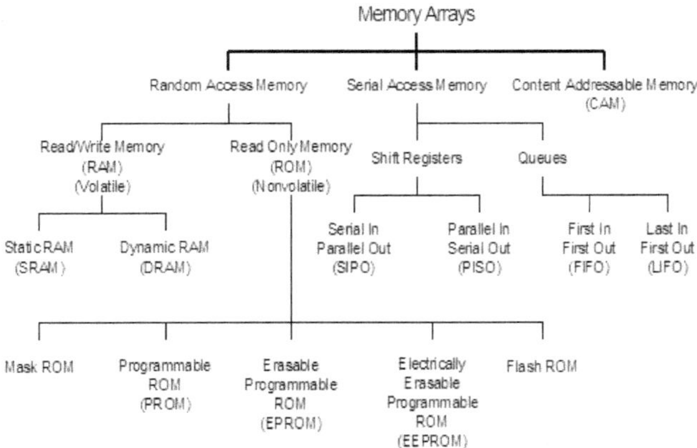

22. Draw the SRAM Cell using CMOS

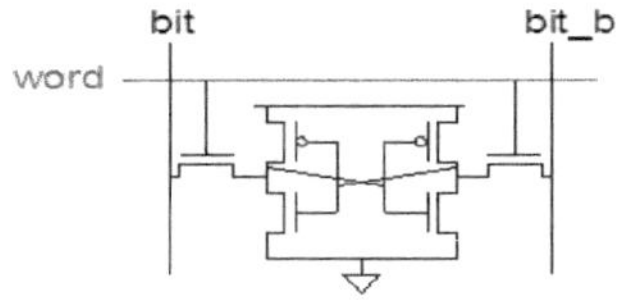

Question Bank

Part-A

1. Draw the circuit diagram for SR latch using NOR gate Version.

2. Draw the circuit diagram for SR latch using CMOS.

3. Draw the circuit diagram for SR latch using NAND gate.

4. Draw the circuit diagram for SR latch using CMOS.

5. Draw the circuit diagram for clocked SR latch using NOR gate Version using CMOS.

6. List different types of Memory Arrays.

7. Draw the Basic building blocks of SRAM Cell.

8. Draw the circuit for D Flip-flop.

9. Draw the circuit for D latch using CMOS.

10. Draw the circuit diagram for clocked CMOS logic circuits.

Part–B

1. Write a brief note on sequencing dynamic circuits.

2. Explain in detail about the principle concepts used in sequential circuits.

3. How do you achieve low power in memory circuits? Explain in detail.

4. Discuss in detail about dynamic RAM.

5. Illustrate the principles of synchronizer.

CHAPTER 4

DESIGNING ARCHITECTURE BUILDING BLOCKS

4.1. Data Path

Data path is a collection of functional units, such as ALU , registers and buses. Along with control unit it composes the central processing unit (CPU). The data path is the core of the processor where all computations are performed. The other blocks in the processor are only supporting units for example store the results produced by data path. Data paths are often arranged in a bit-sliced organization. The interconnecting medium for all the registers inside the processor is the system bus. This bus connects different memory chips and I/O devices to the processor.   The external bus is connected to the internal system bus via the MAR and the MDR registers. The MDR is a bidirectional register implying that it can receive and send data to and from any one of the two internal or external buses. The MAR is a unidirectional register. It receives input from the internal bus and gives its output to the external bus.

The Arithmetic logic unit (ALU) is used for performing arithmetic and logic operations on the data stored in different registers. It is the heart of the microprocessor. The instruction decoder and control logic block decodes the instruction in the IR register and perform the operation. The processor uses all these blocks together to carry out different primary operations such as:

1. Inter Register data transfers

2. Arithmetic or Logical operations

3. Retrieving data from Memory

4. Writing data into the Memory

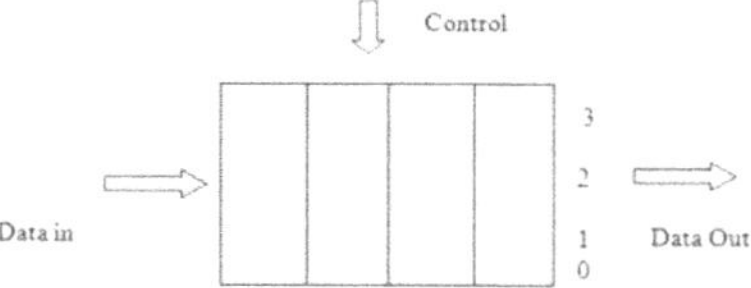

Figure 4.1: Bit Sliced Data Path Organization

Instead of operating on single bit digital signals the data in the processor are arranged in a word based manner. Mostly microprocessor data paths are 32 or 64 bit wide. Signal processing data paths are in compact-disc players, magnetic disk drives and DSL modem. The data path consists of 32 bit slices each operator operates on a single bit. So it is called bit sliced. More effort should be taken on the design of single slice.

4.2. Adder

Addition is the most commonly used arithmetic operation. Careful optimization of the adder is very important. Optimization means manipulation of transistor sizes and circuit topology. One-bit full adder which will be the basis for constructing ripple carry and carry look ahead adders which is explained below.

4.2.1. Full Adder

The operation of full adder is given below. Let A and B are adder inputs. Ci is the carry input S is the sum output and Co is the carry output. Then

$$S = A \oplus B \oplus Ci$$

$$S = \overline{A}\,\overline{B}Ci + \overline{A}\,B\overline{Ci} + A\overline{B}\,\overline{Ci} + ABCi$$

$$Co = AB + BCi + ACi$$

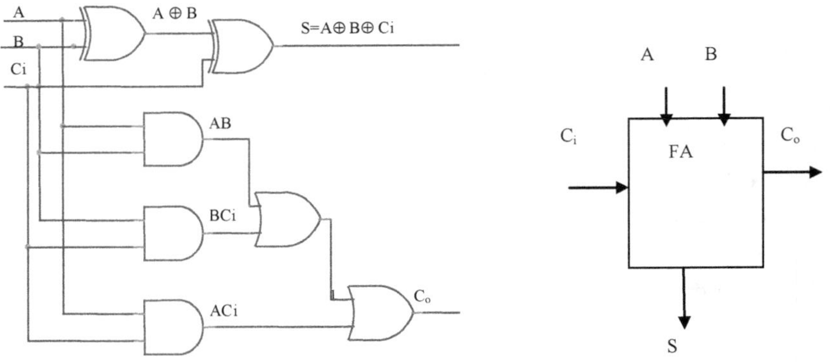

Figure 4.2: Implementation of Full Adder

A	B	Ci	S	Co
0	0	0	0	0
0	0	1	1	0
0	1	0	1	0
0	1	1	0	1
1	0	0	1	0
1	0	1	0	1
1	1	0	0	1
1	1	1	1	1

Figure 4.3: Truth Table of Full Adder

Implementation of Full Adder Using CMOS

We know

$$Co = AB + BCi + ACi$$

$$S = AB.Ci + \overline{Co}\ (A+B+Ci)$$

$$= ABCi + \overline{AB + BCi + ACi}\ (A + B + Ci)$$

Static CMOS implementation is shown below. It requires 25 transistors. It occupies large area and the circuit is slow.

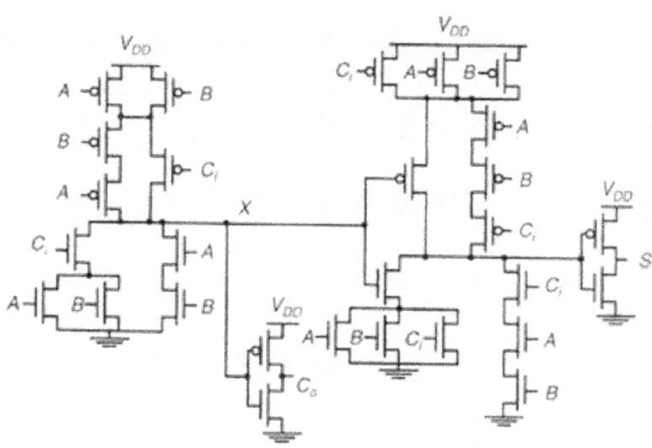

Figure 4.4: Complementary CMOS Implementation of Full Adder

4.2.2.   Ripple Carry Adder

Ripple Carry Adder

Ripple carry adder can be constructed by cascading N full adders. Since the carry ripples from one stage to another it is called ripple carry adder. It can be constructed with full adders connected in cascade, with the carry output from each full adder connected to the carry input of the next full adder in the chain. The interconnection of four full adder circuits forms a 4-bit ripple carry adder. Notice from that the input is from the right side because the first cell traditionally represents the least significant bit (LSB).

Bits A_0 and B_0 in the figure represent the least significant bits of the numbers to be added. The sum output is represented by the bits S_0-S_3.

The delay through the circuit depends up the no. of logic stages traversed and carry ripples from least significant bit (MSB) in all the ways. When designing the full adder cell for a fast ripple carry adder, it is most important to optimize tcarry and tsum where tcarry is equal to propagation delays from Ci to Co and tsum is equal to propagation delay from Ci to S.

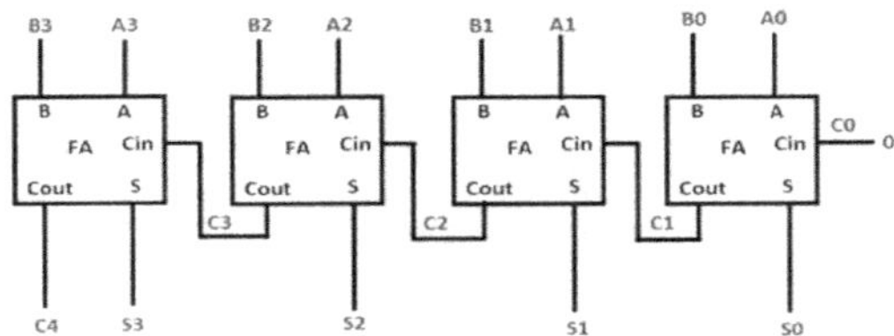

Figure 4.5: 4 Bit Ripple Carry Adder

4.2.3. Transmission Gate based Adder

A full adder can be designed to use multiplexers and XORs. The propagate generate model its implemented using transmission gate is shown below propagate signal is used to select true or complementary value of the input carry as the new sum output.

Based on the propagate signal, the output carry is either set to input carry or either one of inputs A or B.

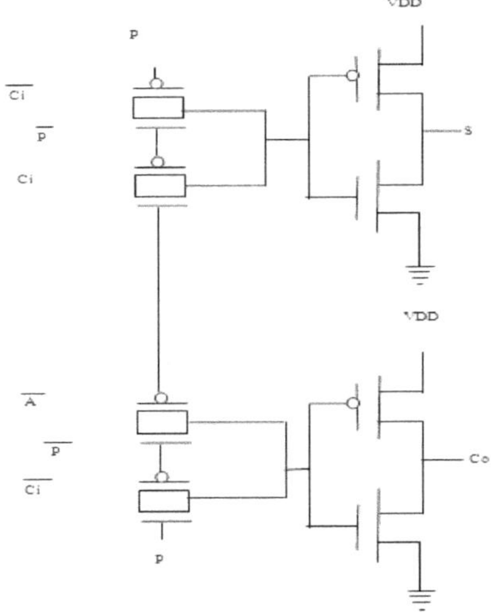

Figure 4.6: Transmission Gate based Adder

4.2.4. Manchester Carry - Chain Adder

Carry propagation circuit in transmission gate based adder can be simplified by adding generate and delete signal. The propagate path is unchanged and it passes Ci to the Co output if the propagate signal is true.

118

G = AB Generate term

D = $\overline{A}\ \overline{B}$ Delete term

P = A⊕B propagate term

If the program conversion is not satisfied, the output is either pulled low by signal or pulled up by $\overline{Gi}$.

In dynamic logic the transmission gate can be replaced by NMOS only pass transistor.

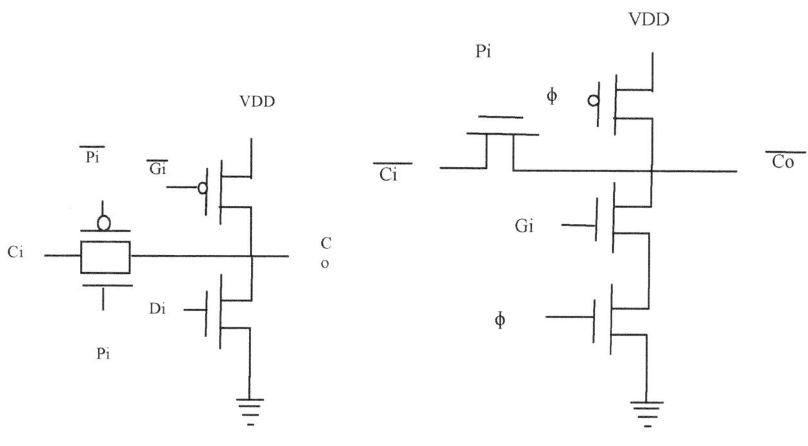

a) Static Implementation b) Dynamic Implementation

Figure 4.7: Manchester Carry Chain Implementation

Manchester carry chain adder uses a cascade of pass transistors to implement the carry chain.

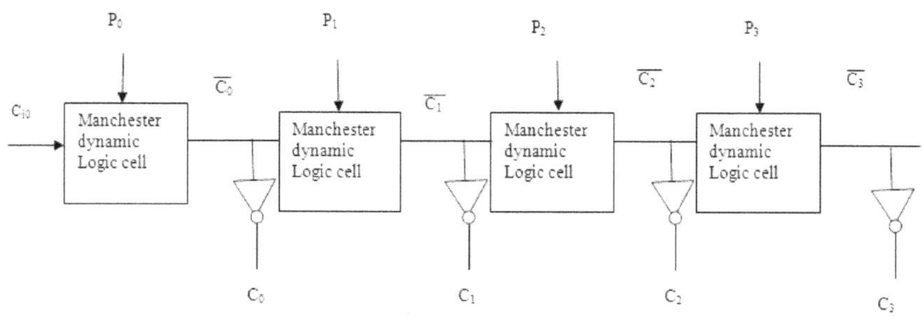

Figure 4.8: Manchester Carry Chain 4 Bit Adder

4.3.   Fast Adders

4.3.1. Carry Look-Ahead Adder

In ripple carry adder, the carry propagation time is the major speed limiting factor. Most other arithmetic operations, e.g. multiplication and division are implemented using several add/subtract steps. Thus, improving the speed of addition will improve the speed of all other arithmetic operations.

Accordingly, reducing the carry propagation delay of adders is of great importance. Different logic design approaches have been employed to overcome the carry propagation problem. One widely used approach employs the principle of carry look-ahead which solves this problem by calculating the carry signals in advance, based on the input signals.

In carry look ahead adder for every bit, the carry and sum outputs are independent of the previous bits. The ripple efforts have been eliminated and the addition time should be independent of the number of bits.

Carry Look ahead adder is based on the fact that a carry signal will be generated in two cases:

1.   When both bits A_i and B_i are 1.
2.   When one of the two bits is 1 and the carry-in (carry of the previous stage) is 1.

To understand the carry propagation problem, let's consider the case of adding two n-bit numbers A and B. G_i is known as the **carry Generate** signal since a carry (C_i+1) is generated whenever $G_i = 1$ regardless of the input carry (C_i)

P_i is known as the **carry propagate** signal since whenever $P_i = 1$, the input carry is propagated to the output carry i.e., $C_{i+1.} = Ci$ (note that whenever $P_i = 1$, $G_i = 0$).

Computing the values of P_i and G_i only depend on the input operand bits $(A_i$ & $B_i)$ as clear from the Figure and equations. Thus, these signals settle to their steady-state value after the propagation through their respective gates. Computed values of the entire P_i are valid on XOR-gate delay after the operands A and B are made valid. Computed values of all the G_i are valid on AND-gate delay after the operands A and B are made valid. The Boolean expression of the carry outputs of various stages can be written as follows:

$$C_1 = G_0 + P_0C_0$$
$$C_2 = G_1 + P_1C_1 = G_1 + P_1 (G_0 + P_0C_0)$$
$$\quad = G_1 + P_1G_0 + P_1P_0C_0$$
$$C_3 = G_2 + P_2C_2 = G_2 + P_2G_1 + P_2P_1G_0 + P_2P_1P_0G_0$$

$$C_4 = G_3 + P_3C_3$$

$$= G_3 + P_3G_2 + P_3P_2G_1 + P_3P_2P_1G_0 + P_3P_2P_1P_0C_0$$

In general, the ith carry output is expressed in the form $C_i = F_i$ (P's, G's, c_0). In other words, each carry signal is expressed as a direct SOP function of C_0 rather than its preceding carry signal. Since the Boolean expression for each output carry is expressed in SOP form, it can be implemented in two-level circuits. The 2-level implementation of the carry signals has a propagation delay of 2 gates, i.e., 2τ. The 4-bit carry look-ahead (CLA) adder consists of 3 levels of logic:

First level: Generates all the P & G signals. Four sets of P & G logic (each consists of an XOR gate and an AND gate) are required. Output signals of this level (P's & G's) will be valid after 1τ.

Second level: The Carry Look-Ahead (CLA) logic block which consists of four 2-level implementation logic circuits. It generates the carry signals (C_1, C2, C3 and C_4) as defined by the above expressions. Output signals of this level (C_1, C_2, C_3 and C_4) will be valid after 3τ.

Third level: Four XOR gates which generates the sum signals (S_i) where $S_i = P_i \oplus C_i$. Output signals of this level will be valid after 4τ.

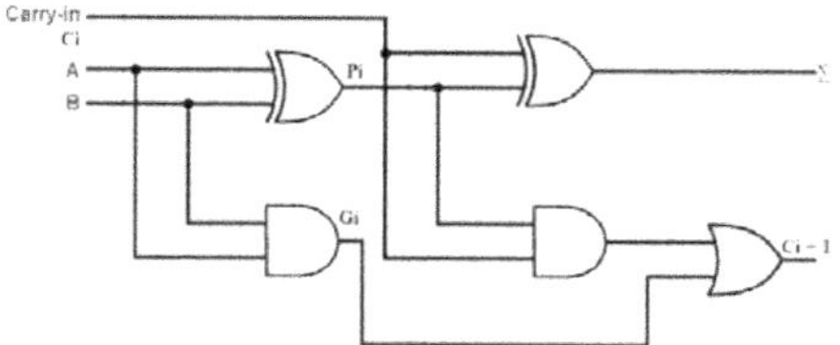

Figure 4.9: Carry-Look Ahead Adder

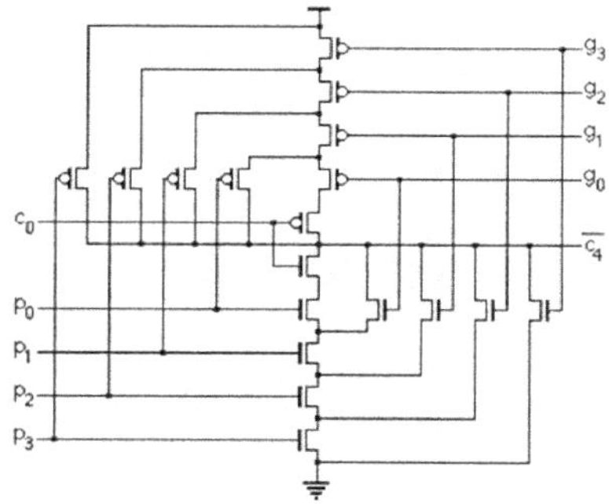

Figure 4.10: Mirror Implementation of Carry Look Ahead Adder

Let G and P are only functions of A and are not dependent on Ci. G is called as generate term and P is called propagate term.

G = AB

P = A⊕B

G= 1 ensures that a carry bit will be generated at Co, independent of Ci. While P=1 guarantees that an incoming carry will propagate to Co.

$$Co\ (G, P) = G + P\ Ci$$
$$= AB + (A⊕B)\ Ci$$
$$S\ (G, P) = P ⊕ Ci$$
$$= A⊕ B⊕ Ci$$

The latency associated with ripple carry adder can be reduced by using carry - Look-Ahead adder.

General expression for carry out bit is,

$$Cn+1 = Gn+ Pn.Cn$$

Where $Gn = an.\ bn$

$Pn = an⊕bn$

$Sn = Pn ⊕Cn$

The structure of carry Look ahead adder is shown below.

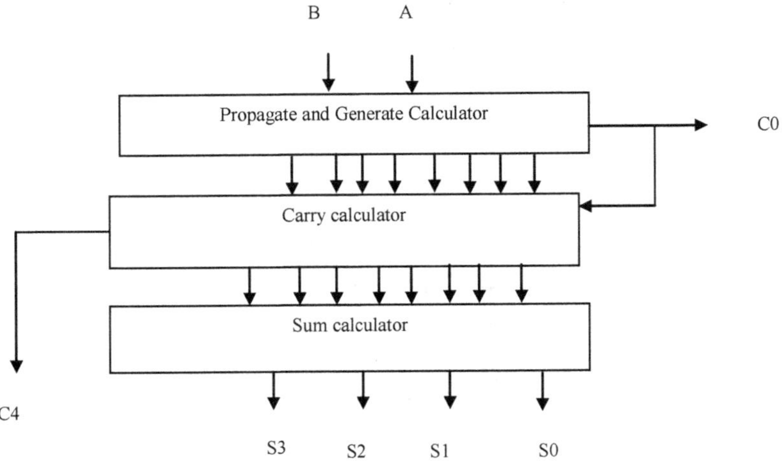

Figure 4.11: Carry Look Ahead Adder

Carry Look Ahead Adder reduces both area and delay. Full adder implementation requires 24 transistors. Ripple carry adder is applied for the implementation of adder with small word length. Ripple carry adders are not used in desktop and super computers because most desktop computers use word lengths of 32 bit and super computers require word length of up to 128 bits.

Carry Bypass Adder (Carry Skip Adder)

The propagation delay of carry bypass adder is

$$t_p = t_{setup} + M t_{carry} + \left(\frac{N}{M} - 1 \right) t_{bypass} + (M-1)\, t_{carry} + t_{setup}$$

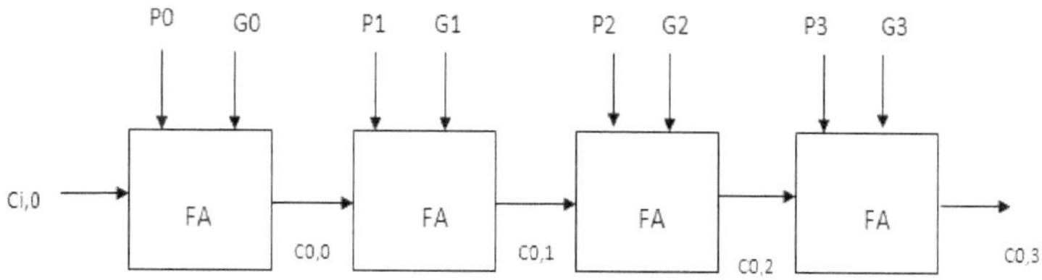

a) Carry Propagation

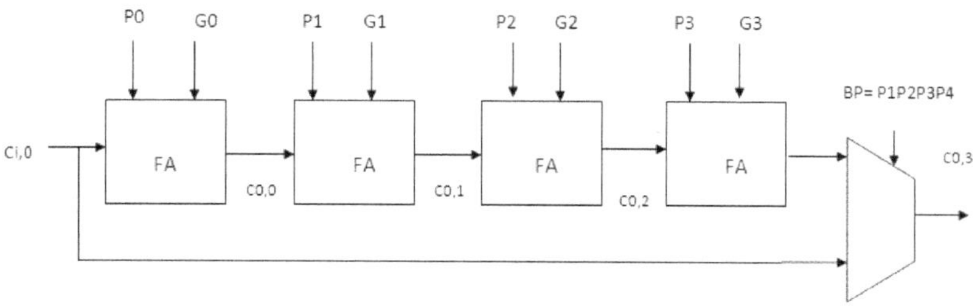

b) Carry Propagation and bypass adder

Figure 4.12: Carry Bypass Adder

Inputs are defined as

4 bits of C0 are C0,3 C0,2 C0,1 C0,0

4 bits of Ak are A3   A2   A1   A0

4 bits of Bk are B3   B2   B1   B0

Suppose the values of Ak and Bk (K=0....3) are such that all propagate signals Pk (k=0....3) are high level. Incoming carry Ci,0=1 propagates under these conditions through the complete adder chain and causes an output carry Co,3=1.

In other words of $(P_0P_1P_2P_3=1)$ then,

$$Co, 3 = Ci, o$$

Else either Delete or Generate occurred.

These concepts can be used to speed up the operation of the adder.

Carry propagation and the incoming carry is forwarded immediately to the next block through the bypass transistor Mb -hence the name bypass adder of carry-skip adder.

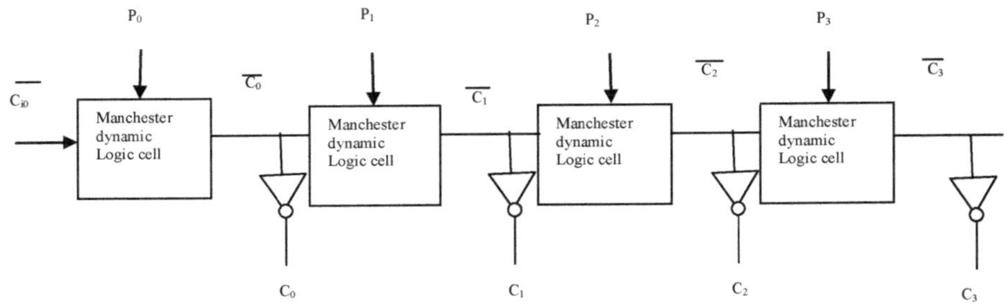

Figure 4.13: Manchester Carry-Chain Implementation of Bypass-Adder

4.3.2. *Logarithmic Look-Ahead Adder*

The implementation of Carry look ahead adder for N bits uses N+ 1 parallel branches with up to N+ 1 transistors in the stack. The carry look ahead computation has been limited to up to bits in practice. To build fast adder, it is necessary to organize carry propagation and generation into exclusive trees.

$$C0, 0 = G0 + P0\ Ci,0$$
$$C0,1 = G1+ P1\ C0,0$$
$$C0,1 = G1+P1\ (G0+P0\ Ci,0)$$
$$C0,1 = G1+P1G0+P1P0\ Ci,0$$
$$C0,1 = (a1+P1+G0) + (P1, P0)\ Ci,0$$
$$C0,1 = G1{:}0 + P1{:}0\ Ci,0$$

In the same manner

$$C0,2 = G2 + P2\ C0,1$$
$$C0,3= G3{:}\ 2 + P3{:}2\ C0,1$$

G0:j and Pi:j denote, generate and carry propagate functions respectively for a group of bits. Therefore we call them block generate and propagate signals.

G3: 2 = G3 + P3 G2

4.4. Divider

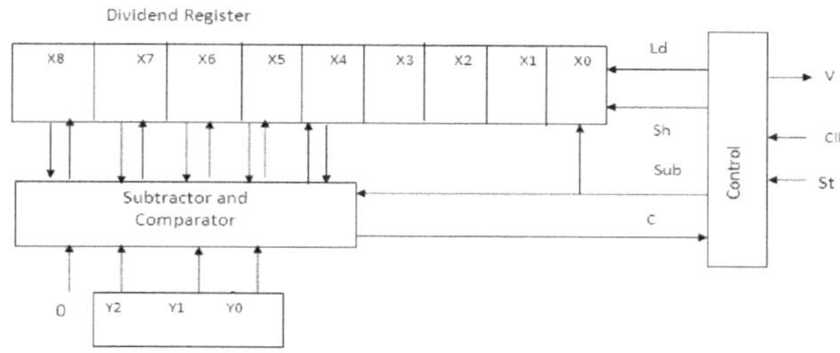

Figure 4.14: Structure of Divider

4.5. Accumulator

An accumulator is an 8-bit register that is a part of ALU (Arithmetic Logic Unit) of a processor. It is used for temporary storage of 8-bit data and to perform arithmetic operations like addition, subtraction, multiplication, division or logical operations like AND, OR, XOR etc. The result of operation is stored in accumulator. Although addition and multiplication are two different operations, they can be performed in parallel. By the time the multiplier is computing the product, accumulator can accumulate the product of the previous multiplications.

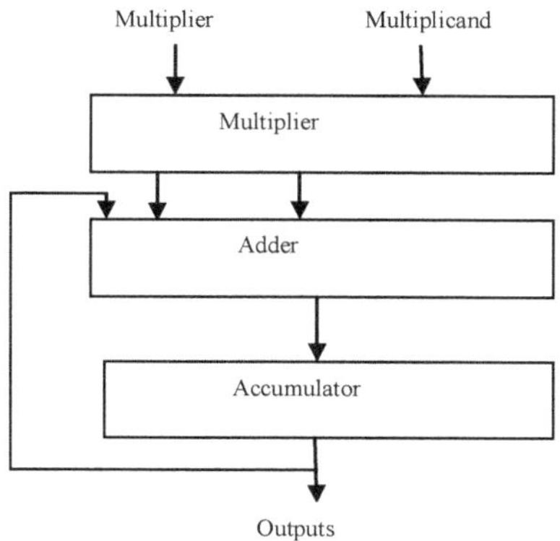

Figure 4.15: Block Diagram of MAC

4.6. Binary Multiplier

Multipliers are the important block in digital signal processors. Multipliers need addition operator to find the result. The multiplier is multiplied by each bit of the multiplicand, starting from the least significant bit. The result of each such multiplication forms a partial product. Successive partial products are shifted one bit to the left. The product is obtained by adding these shifted partial products. Consider an example of multiplication of two numbers, say A and B (2 bits each).The output $C = A * B$.

The first partial product is formed by multiplying the **B_1B_0** by **A_0**. The multiplication of two bits such as **A_0** and **B_0** produces a 1 if both bits are 1; otherwise it produces a 0 like an AND operation. So the partial products can be implemented with AND gates. The second partial product is formed by multiplying the **B_1B_0** and **A_1** and is shifted one position to the left.

	A_1	A_0	
	B_1	B_0	
	A_0B_1	A_0B_0	
A_1B_1	A_1B_0		
C_3	C_2	C_1	C_0

Figure 4.16: 2 bit Multiplication Process

The two partial products are added with two half adders (HA). Usually there are more bits in the partial products, and then it will be necessary to use FAs.

The least significant bit of the product does not have to go through an adder, since it is formed by the output of the first AND gate.

A binary multiplier with more bits can be constructed in a similar manner.

Consider the example of multiplying two numbers, say A (3-bit number) and B (4-bit number). Each bit of A (the multiplier) is AND with each bit of B (the multiplicand) as shown in the Figure.

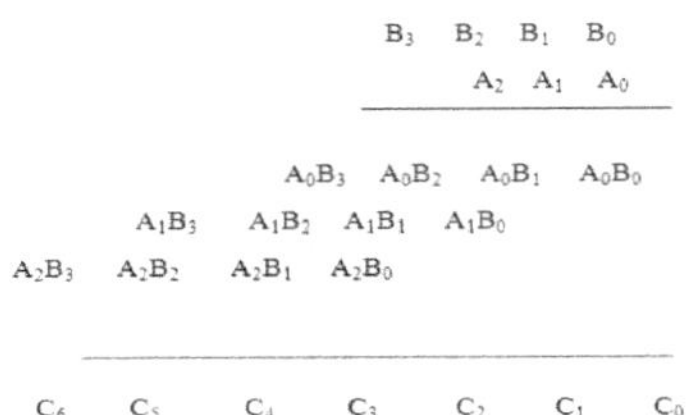

Figure 4.17: 4 bit* 3 Bit Multiplication Process

The binary output in each level of AND gates are added in parallel with the partial product of the previous level to form a new partial product. The last level produces the final product.

Since J = 3 and K = 4, 12 (J x K) AND gates and two 4-bit ((J-1) K-bit) adders are needed to produce a product of seven (J + K) bits.

Note that **0** applied at the most significant bit of augends of first 4-bit adder because the least significant bit of the product does not have to go through an adder.

For example the multiplication of 101011 with 1100 is given below.

```
      10 10 11    Multiplier
         11 00    Multiplier
      ---------
       000000
      000000        partial
     101011         products
    101011
    ----------
    1000000100
```

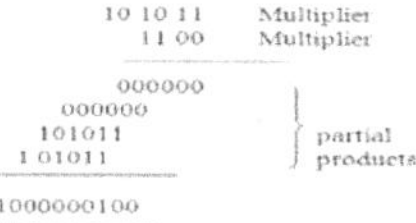

Figure 4.18: Binary Multiplication-An Example

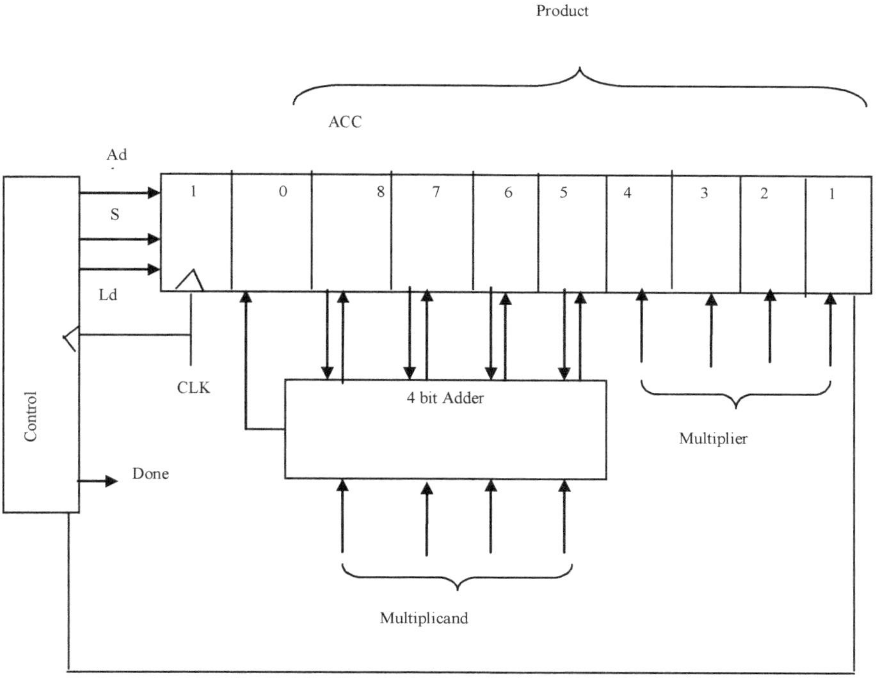

Figure 4.19: Structure of Multiplier

The multiplication of two inputs that are M and N bits uses N bit adder. The shift and add algorithm for multiplication adds together M partial products. Each partial product is generated by multiplying the multiplicand with a bit of a multiplier. AND gate is used for implementation of partial product generation.

Partial Product Generation

Each row in the partial product array is either a copy of the multiplicand or a row off zeros. Optimization of partial products generation leads to reduction in products generation which leads to reduction in delay and area. To reduce the number of partial products terms, Booths algorithm is used. Reducing the number of partial products is equivalent to reducing the number of additions, which leads to speed up as well as area reduction.

Partial Product Accumulation

In multiplication, after the partial products are generated they must be summed. Accumulation of partial products uses a number of adders.

4.7. Array Multiplier

The multiplication of x and y array multiplier results in product z.

$x \rightarrow x_3\, x_2 x_1\, x_0$

$y \rightarrow y_3 y_2 y_1 y_0$

$z = z_7 z_6\, z_5\, z_4\, z_3\, z_2\, z_1\, z_0$

The generation of N partial product requires N*M two bit AND gates, it requires N-1, M bit address to add partial products. The shifting of the partial products does not require any logic. Transistor sizing yields the increase in performance of multiplier.

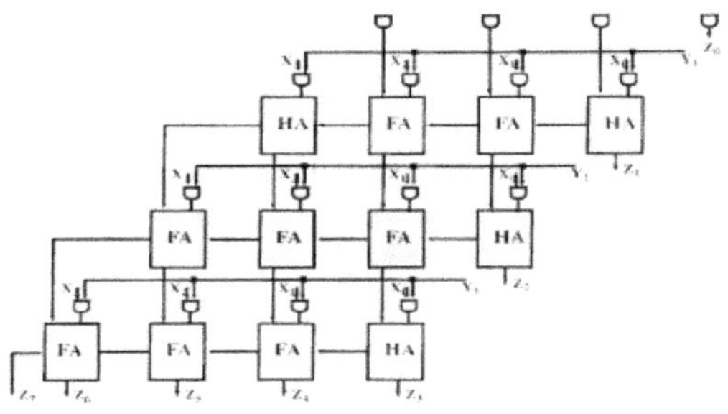

Figure 4.20: 4*4 Bit Array Multiplier for Unsigned Numbers

A more efficient realization can be obtained by noticing that the multiplication result does not change when the output carry bits are passed diagonally downwards instead of only to the right. The resulting multiplier is called **carry save multiplier** found by **Wallace**. Here carry bits are not immediately added. In the final stage, carries and sums are merged in a fast carry-look ahead adder. It slightly increases area. But the propagation delay is reduced.

4.8.   Wallace-Tree Multiplier

In 4x4 multiplier, the partial products are shown in Figure 4.21. The partial products are rearranged into tree form. The column 3 in the carry only has to add four bits. All the other columns are little complex. Full Adder is also called 3-2 compressor because the input for full adder is 3 bits and outputs are sum and carry. Three FAs and three HAs are used for the reduction process compared with six FAs and six HAs in a carry save multiplier. Final addition for completing multiplication is to combine the result in Final adder. A carry look ahead adder is the preferred option, if all input bits arrive at the same time to the adder. For pipelined multipliers other adder topologies can be preferred.

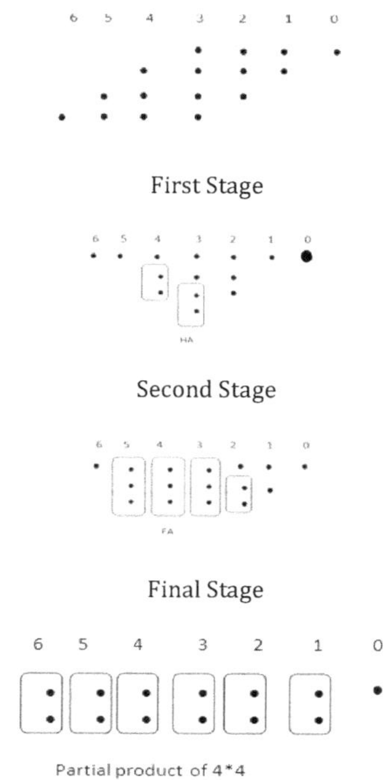

Figure 4.21: Partial Product of 4x4 Multiplier

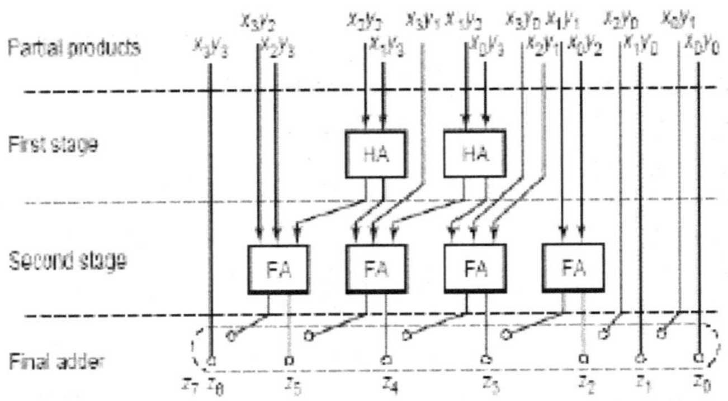

Figure 4.22: Wallace Tree for Four Bit Multiplier

4.9.   Shifter

The shift operation is another essential arithmetic operation. Add and shift method can be preferred for multiplications by constant numbers. In hardware a data word shifting to left or right over a constant amount is used for multiplication. Depending on the control signals, the input word is either shifted left or right or else it remains unchanged. Multi bit shifter can be constructed by cascading a number of blocks like this.

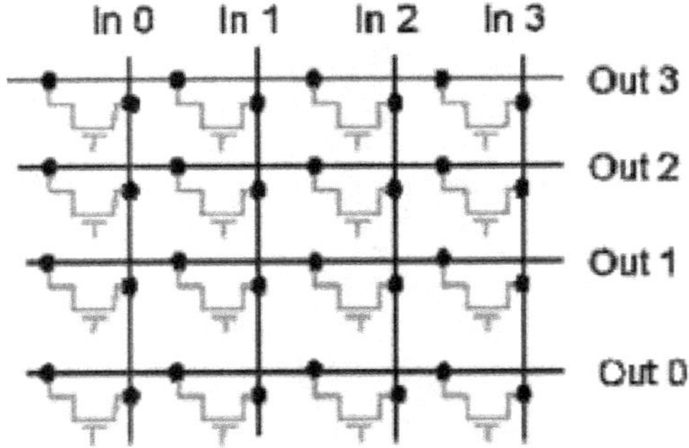

Figure 4.23: Implementation of 4 Bit Shifter

A Barrel Shifter is a logic component that perform shift or rotate operations. Barrel shifters are applicable for digital signal processing. This component design is for natural size (4, 8, 16…) .Barrel shifters perform shift right ,logical, rotate right, shift left logical, and rotate left operations depending on the instantiation parameters. The left and right operation is implemented through inversion of the input and output vectors, so the basic multiplexing function can perform both operations. The structure of a barrel shifter is shown below. It consists of an array of transistors in which the number of rows equals to the word length of the data and number of columns equals to maximum shift width. For example select both length equal to four. The control wires are routed diagonally through the array. The propagation delay is theoretically constant and independent of shift value or shifter size. Barrel shifter needs a control wire for every shift bit. Four bit shifter needs four control signals. In a processor the required shift value normally comes in an encoded binary format which is more compact. Shifting the input over three bits needs the control bit 11.

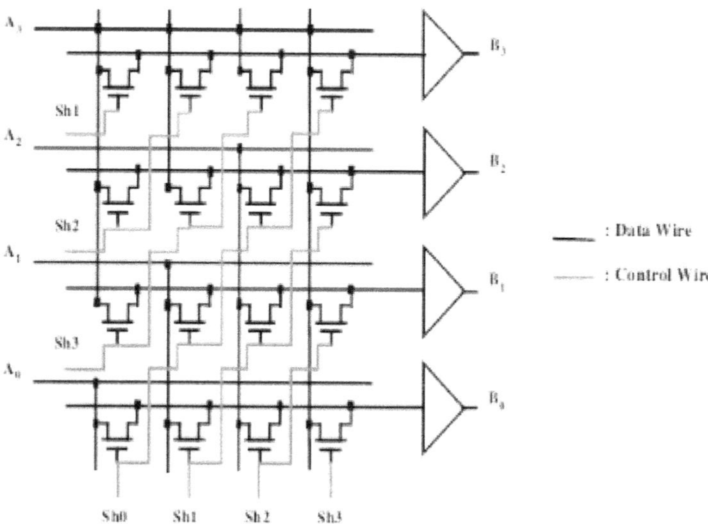

Figure 4.24: Barrel Shifter

4.10. Speed and Area Trade-OFF

- Digital circuit design is a trade-off between area, speed and power requirement. The following fig shows a graph between normalized area and speed of some of the address as the function of number of bits. Select the right structure before starting an optimization. Optimizations at higher levels such as logic or architectural level can generate good results. Most of the optimizations are done through the critical timing path. Tools are available to calculate critical paths.

The important points to be followed is,

- Circuit size is not only determined by number and size of the transistors but also by other factors such as wiring and number of vias and contacts.
- Power and speed can be traded off through a choice of circuit sizing, supply voltages and transistor thresholds.

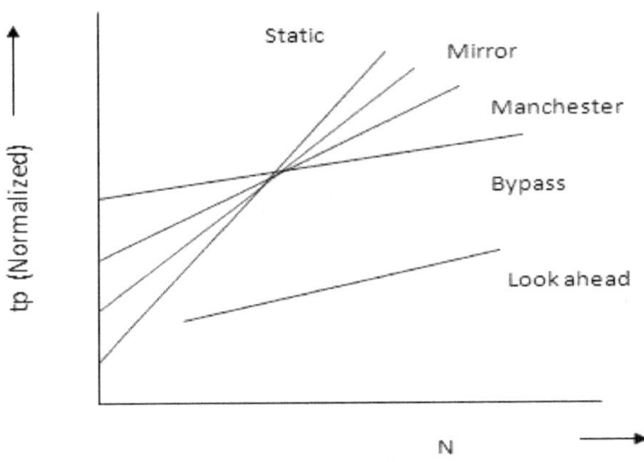

Figure 4.25: Propagation Delay Vs Number of Bits

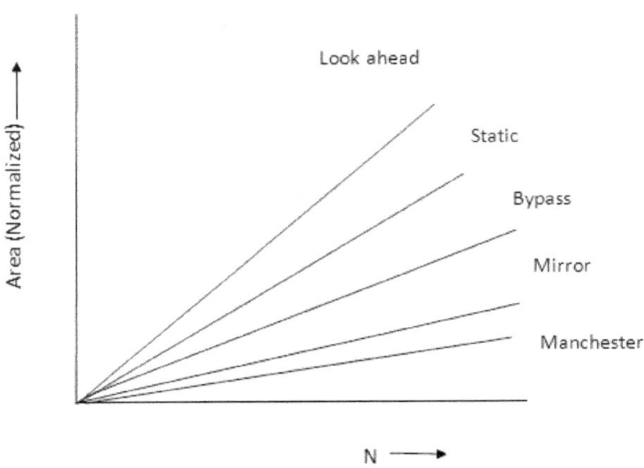

Figure 4.26: Area Vs Number of Bits

2 Mark Questions with Answer

1. Define a data path.

   Data path is the core of a processor. It is where all computations are performed. They are generally arranged in a bit sliced organization.

2. What is meant by bit-sliced data path organization?

   Data path is where all computations are performed in a processor. They are arranged in a bit–sliced organization. Instead of operating on single bit digital signals, the data in a processor is arranged in a word **based** fashion. A 32 bit processor operates on data words that are 32 bit wide. Since the same operation has to be performed on each bit of the data word, the data path consists of 32 identical slices, each of them operating on a single bit. So the name bit sliced. Data path designer can concentrate on the design of a single slice that is repeated 32 times.

3. Write down the Expression for the total propagation delay in an n bit carry bypass Adder.
$$Tp = tset\ up + M\ tcarry + (N/M\text{-}1)\ tbypass + M\ tcarry + tsum.$$

4. What is the total time delay for a ripple carry Adder?
$$Tadder = (N\text{-}1)\ tcarry + tsum.$$

5. List the different considerations for designing a Ripple carry adder.
   1. Propagation delay of ripple carry adder is linearly proportional to N.
   2. It is important to optimize tcarry than tsum.
   3. Inverting all i/ps to a full adder results in inverted values for all o/ps.

6. What are the draw backs of a static adder circuit?
   1. Consumes large area.
   2. Circuit is slow.

7. Why is static adder circuit slow?

   A static adder circuit is slow as,

   1. Long chains of series PMOS transistors are present in both carry & Sum generation circuit.
   2. Intrinsic load capacitance of the Co signal is large and consists of 2 diffusion & 6 gate capacitances plus the wiring g capacitances.
   3. Carry generation circuit requires 2 inverting stages per bit.
   4. Sum generation circuit requires an extra logic stage.

8. What is the advantage of Dynamic adder design?

   Reduced capacitance of dynamic circuitry results results in substantial speed up over static implementation.

9.   What is a Manchester carry chain adder?

It uses a cascade of pass transistors to implement the carry chain. Propagate & Generate signals are generated using pass transistor logic. The capacitance per node on the carry chain is very small & equals only 4 diffusion capacitances.

10. Why is carry bypass Adder called so?

When the bypass control signal is set to '1', the incoming carry is forwarded immediately to the next block through a bypass transistor.

11. Give the expression for the carry output of an n bit carry look ahead adder.

$$C_o(k) = G_k + C_o(k-1)$$

12. What is the importance of linear carry select Adder?

The linear dependencies present in a ripple carry adder is avoided in linear carry select adder, by anticipating both possible values of the carry i/p and evaluate the result for both possibilities in advance.

13. Why is the propagation delay in a carry select Adder is linearly proportional to N?

It is because the block select signal that selects between 0&1 solutions still has to ripple through all stages in worst case.

14. List the advantages of two phase clocking scheme.

    1.   No chance of race conditions occurring in the circuit.

    2.   No timing errors due to races or Hazards or clock skew.

    3.   Two phase clocking schemes are popular due to its simplicity & reliability.

    4.   Design procedures are also simple.

15. What are the major problems associated with the single phase clocking scheme?

    1.   Race or hazards.

    2.   Timing errors

16. What are the advantages of AOI implementation of two level logic functions?

Construction of AOI cells is particularly efficient using CMOS technology where the total number of transistor gates can be reduced compared to the same construction using NAND logic or NOR logic.

17. Name the two phases of operation in a dynamic CMOS logic

    1.   Precharge.

    2.   Evaluate.

18. What is two phase clocking?

Inverting a single clock can lead to skew problems. Employ two non-overlapping clocks for master and slave sections of a flip-flop. Thus we can have between one and four clock lines to route around the chip

19. How data path can be implemented in VLSI system?

A data path is best implemented in a bit –sliced fashion. A single layout is used respectively for every bit in the data word. This regular approach eases the design effort and results in fast and dense layouts.

20. Comment on performance of ripple carry adder.

A ripple carry adder has a performance that is linearly proportional to the number of bits. Circuit optimizations concentrate on reducing the delay of the carry path. A number of circuit topologies exist providing that careful optimization of the circuit topology and the transistor sizes helps to reduce the capacitance on the carry bit.

21. What is the logic of adder for increasing its performance?

Adder structures use logic optimizations to increase the performance (carry bypass, carry select, carry look ahead). Performance increase comes at the cost area.

22. What is multiplier circuit?

A multiplier is nothing more than a collection of cascaded adders. Critical path is far more complex and optimizations are different compared to adders.

23. Which factors dominate the performance of programmable shifter?

The performance and the area of a programmable shifter are dominated by the wiring.

24. What is meant by data path?

A datapath is a functional unit, such as arithmetic logic units or multipliers that perform data processing operations, registers and buses. Along with the control unit it composes the central processing unit.

25. Write down the expression for worst-case delay for RCA.

$$t = (n\text{-}1)\ tc + ts$$

26. Write down the expression to obtain delay for N-bit carry bypass adder.

$$tadder = tsetup + Mtcarry + (N/M\text{-}1)t\ bypass + (M\text{-}1)tcarry + tsum$$

27. Define Braun multiplier.

The simplest multiplier is the Braun multiplier. All the partial products are computed in parallel, and then collected through a cascade of Carry Save Adders. The completion time is limited by the depth of the carry save array, and by the carry propagation in the adder. This multiplier is suitable for positive operands.

28. Why we go to Booth's algorithm?

Booth algorithm is a method that will reduce the number of multiplicand multiples. For a given number of ranges to be represented, a higher representation radix leads to fewer digits.

29. Draw the truth table for Modified booth's algorithm.

X2n+1	X2n	X2n-1	f(2n)	f(2n)Y
0	0	0	0	0
0	0	1	1	Y
0	1	0	1	Y
0	1	1	2	2Y
1	0	0	-2	-2Y
1	0	1	-1	-Y
1	1	0	-1	-Y
1	1	1	0	0

30. List the different types of shifter.

1. Array shifter

2. Barrel shifter

3. Logarithmic shifter

Question Bank

Part-A

1. Design logic to reduce the number of generated partial products by half for Multiplication.
2. Describe Vector merging adder.
3. What is Wallace tree multiplier?
4. Give a note on barrel Shifters.
5. Create a partial product selection table using modified booth's recoding.
6. Identify the Arithmetic circuits in the design of processors.
7. What are the Arithmetic structures derived from a full adder?
8. List the Advantages of dual supply approach.
9. Analyze the Dynamic voltage scaling and list its advantages.
10. List the uses of Clock gating?
11. Create a schematic for Sleep transistors used on both supply and ground.
12. Give a neat sketch on Manchester carry gates.
13. Explain Bit sliced data path organization.
14. Explain the inverting property of full adder.

Part-B

1.
    (i) Describe ripple carry adder and derive the worst case delay with example. (12)

    (ii) Describe the inversion property of full adder. (4)

2. Classify circuit design considerations of full adder and explain.

    (i) Mirror adder. (8)

    (ii) Transmission gate adder. (8)

3. List the logic design considerations of binary adder and explain.

    (i) Carry skip adder. (8)

    (ii) Carry save adder. (8)

4.
    (i) Illustrate the concepts of monolithic and logarithmic look ahead adder.

    (ii) Illustrate the concepts of monolithic and logarithmic look ahead adder. (8)

5. Define shifter and give a short note.

    (i) Barrel shifter. (8)

    (ii) Carry save multiplier. (8)

6.

   (i)   Design the arithmetic logic unit (ALU) of 64 bit high end microprocessor and
         arithmetic operators involved in design.   (12)

   (ii) Give a short note on Logarithmic shifter.   (4)

7.

   (i)   Summarize the methods involved in run time power management.   (12)

   (ii) Compare the difference between DVS and DTS.   (4)

   (iii) The implementation of a look ahead adder in dynamic logic.   (10)

   (iv) Explain the advantages of Carry bypass adder compared to other adders.   (6)

8.

   (i)   Give a note on linear carry select adder.   (10)

   (ii) Discuss the data paths in digital processor architectures.   (6)

CHAPTER 5

IMPLEMENTATION STRATEGIES FOR DIGITAL ICs

Reducing the system size through integration is the major objective in most consumer applications. The design cost can be reduced substantially by using advanced techniques which compromise performance but minimize design time.

The cost of semiconductor fabrication is the sum of two components.

1. Non recurring Expense (NRE), which is incurred only once for a design.
2. Production cost per part which is a function of the process completely and design area.

5.1. Implementation Techniques

The different techniques of implementation of digital integrated circuit are given below.

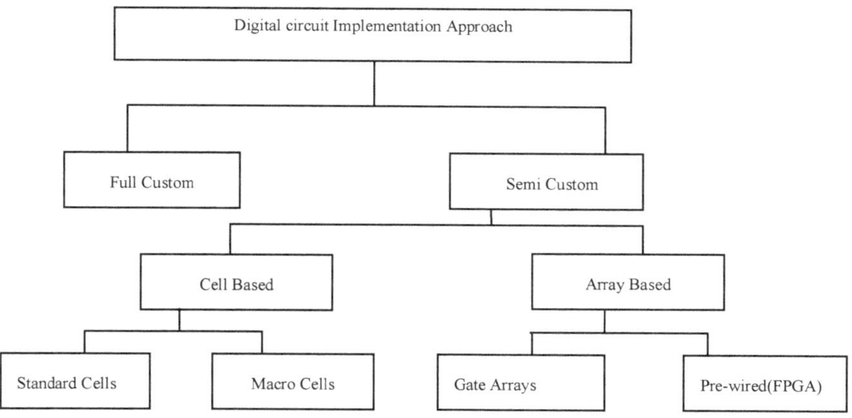

Figure 5.1: Implementation Approaches for Digital Integrated Circuits

5.1.1. Full Custom Design

A full custom IC includes few logic cells customized and all masks layers customized. A microprocessor is an example of a full custom IC. Designers spend many hours, to design full custom IC.Full custom ICs are most expensive to manufacture and to design. The amount of design automation in the custom design process is minimal. If cost is not the prime factor then the full custom design is selected. Full-custom design is a methodology for designing integrated circuits by specifying the layout of each individual transistor and the interconnection between them. In Full-Custom ASIC an engineer designs some or all of the logic cells circuits or layout.

5.1.2. Semi Custom Design (ASIC)

Since the full custom design approach is more expensive, a wide variety of design approaches have been introduced. Alternative to full custom design include various forms of semi custom design, such as the repetition of small transistor sub circuits; one such methodology is the use of standard cell libraries. In semicustom ASICs, all of the logic cells are predesigned and some of the mask layers are customized using predesigned cells from a cell library simplifies the complexity of design.

5.2. Types of Semicustom Design

Two types of semicustom based IC design is standard-cell-based ASIC and gate-array based ASIC.

5.2.1. Cell based Approach

Cell based Approach reduces the design time. It reduces the implementation effect by reusing a limited library of cells. The cells need to be designed and verified for a given technology. They can be reused many times.

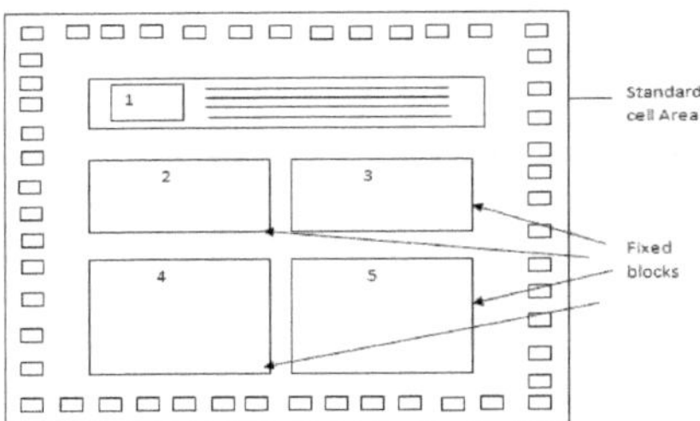

Figure 5.2: Cell based Approach

The types of Cell based Approach are:

1. Standard-Cell based ASIC

Cell based ASIC cell based IC uses predesigned logic cells predesigned logic cells are called standard cells. Examples of logic cells are AND gate, OR gate, multiplex and FFs. CBIC architecture consists of row of standard cells. The designer defines only the placement of the standard cells and the interconnection. The advantage of standard cell based ASIC is that designers save time, money and reduce risk by using a predesigned cell library. Each and every transistor in cell library can be designed to maximize speed and minimize area. The disadvantages are the time or expense of designing or buying the standard cell library. The important feature of it is all mask layers are customized. Standard cells are designed to fit in the cell array. In cell based ASIC we can change the transistor sizes in the standard cell to optimize speed and performance.

2. Macro Cells and Mega Cells based Approach

Macro Cells

Standardizing at the logic gate level is inefficient for more complex structures such as multipliers, memories and Microprocessors. An efficient implementation can be obtained by capturing the specific nature of these blocks. Cells that contain a complexity that surpasses what is found in a typical standard cell library are called macro cells.

Hard Macro

Hard Macro is a predetermined physical design. It represents a full custom design of a requested function. The location of the transistors and the wiring within the module is fixed.

Advantages: It can be reused over and over in different designs. The reuse reduces initial design cost.

Disadvantages: For every new technology a major redesign of the block is necessary.

Soft Macro

It represents a module with a given function but without a specific physical implementation. The placement and wiring of soft macro may vary from instance to instance.

Soft macro cell generators are available in different styles depending on the type of the function. If the desired function and values for requested parameters are given to macro generators, they will produce a net list.

More complex circuits are built by using reusable building blocks. These modules are purchased from third party vendors. Macros distributed in this style are called intellectual property (IP) module.

Advantages: Soft macros can be ported over a wide range of technologies and processes.

5.2.2. Array Based ASICs

In gate array abbreviated GA; the transistors are predefined on the silicon wafer. The logic cells in the gate array are called macros. Only top few layers of metal which define the interconnection between transistors are defined by the designer using custom mask.

Pre diffused (mask-programmable) and Pre-wired are the two types of array based approach.

5.3. Types of Array Based ASICs

5.3.1. Pre Diffused (Mask-Programmable)

Different types of Pre Diffused array based ASIC are:

1. Channeled Gate Array

In channeled gate array space between rows of transistor are used for wiring. Features of channeled gate array are (i) only the interconnect is customized ii) The interconnect uses predefined spaces between rows of base cells.

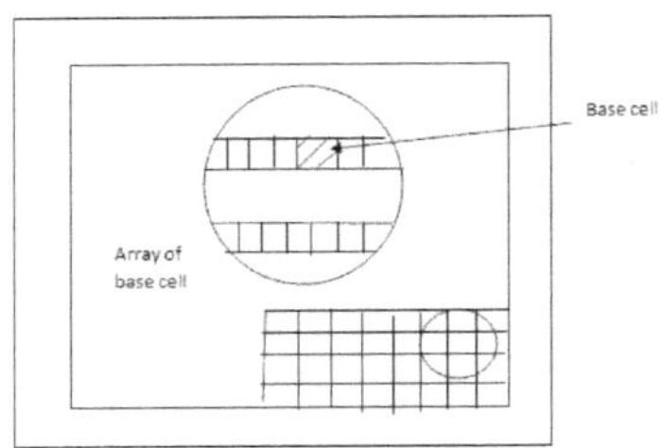

Figure 5.3: Channeled Gate Array

2. Channelless Gate Array

The amount of logic that can be implemented in a given silicon area is higher for channel less gate array. Customizing the contact layer in a channelless gate array allows increase in density of gate array. The routing on the channelless gate array uses rows of unused transistor.

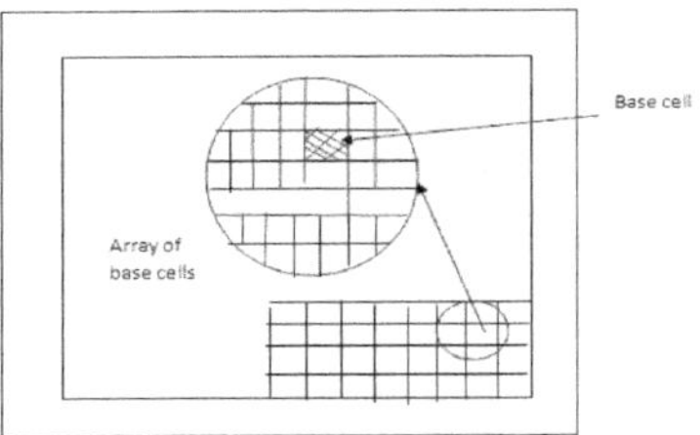

Figure 5.4: Channelless Gate Array

5.4. FPGA

A Field-programmable gate array (FPGA) is a semiconductor device containing programmable logic components called "logic blocks", and programmable interconnects. Logic blocks can be programmed to perform the function of basic logic gates such as AND, and XOR, or more complex combinational functions such as decoders or mathematical functions. In most FPGAs, the logic blocks also include memory elements, which may be simple flip-flops or more complete blocks of memory. A hierarchy of programmable interconnects allows logic blocks to be interconnected as needed by the system designer, somewhat like a one-chip programmable breadboard.

Logic blocks and interconnects can be programmed by the customer or designer, after the FPGA is manufactured to implement any logical function-hence the name "field-programmable". FPGAs are usually slower than application-specific integrated circuit. But their advantages include a shorter time to market, ability to re-program in the field to fix bugs, and lower non-recurring engineering costs. Vendors can sell cheaper, less flexible versions of their FPGAs.

A step above the PLD in complexity is the field-programmable gate array (FPGA). There is very little difference between an FPGA and PLD. An FPGA is usually just larger and more complex than PLD. FPGAs are the newest member of the ASIC family and are rapidly growing in importance, replacing TTL in microelectronic systems. None of the mask layers are customized. It uses an efficient method for programming the basic logic cells and interconnect.

FPGA Design Advantages

- **Faster time to market:** No layout, masks or other manufacturing steps are needed for FPGA design. Readymade FPGA is available to burn our HDL code.

- **Simpler design cycle:** This is due to software that handles much of the routing, placement, and timing. Manual intervention is less. This FPGA design flow eliminates the complex and time-consuming floor planning, place and route and timing analysis.

- **Field Reprogrammability:** A new bit stream can be uploaded remotely, instantly. FPGA can be reprogrammed in a snap while an ASIC can take more than 4-6 weeks to make the same changes.

- **Reusability:** Reusability of FPGA is the main advantage. Prototype of the design can be implemented on FPGA which could be verified for almost accurate results so that it can be implemented on an ASIC. If design has faults, the HDL code is changed to generate a bit stream. Modern FPGAs are reconfigurable both partially any dynamically.

- FPGAs are good for prototyping and limited production. Generally FPGAs are used for lower speed, lower complexity and lower volume designs. But today's FPGAs even run at 500MHZ with superior performance.

- Good for low quantity production. As quantity increases cost per product increases compared to the ASIC implementation.

FPGA Design Disadvantages

- Power consumption in FPGA is more.
- We have to use only resources available in the FPGA. Thus FPGA limits the design size.

5.5. VLSI Design Flow

The following figure clearly depicts the VLSI design flow in a flowchart representation. Design entry describes the designs in Hardware description languages (HDLs) such as verilog and VHDL. The design represented in HDL is synthesized to get the gate level netlist. The design represented in HDL code hardware can be implemented on an FPGA board only if, it is synthesizable. The functional check, timing checks and the power analysis checks are included in the verification. After successful synthesis and behavioral simulation, the design can be moved to the implementation stage. During the implementation stage, combinational delays associated with the logic components are considered and the design is again simulated to check for any timing violations. Then, the EDA tool place routes the design on the target FPGA device and provides the designer with exact report with respect to routing delays and combinational delays.

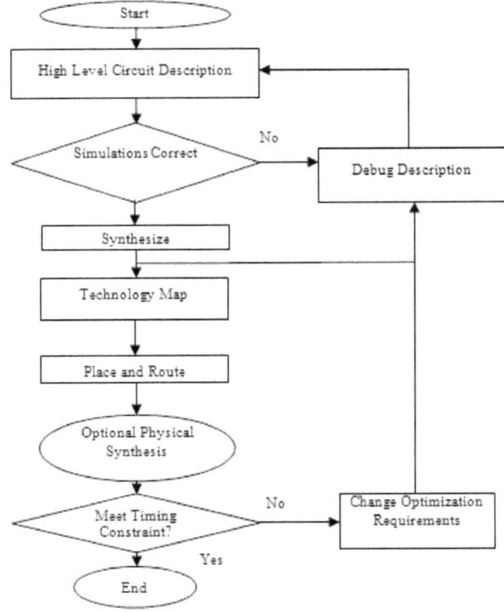

Figure 5.5: VLSI Design Flow

5.6.   ASIC Design Flow

An Application-Specific Integrated Circuit (ASIC) is an integrated circuit designed for a particular use rather that intended for general-purpose use. Processors, RAM, ROM, etc are examples of ASICs. The Steps to design an ASIC is given below.

Design Entry: Enter the design either using a hardware description language (HDL) or schematic entry.

Logic synthesis: Use a logic synthesis tool to produce a netlist.

System partitioning: Divide a large system into small sized modules

Pre Layout simulation: It is used to check if the design functions correctly or not.

Floor planning: In floor planning using an algorithm the blocks of the netlist are arranged on the chip.

Placement: The locations of cells in a block are decided.

Routing: An efficient algorithm is used to connect the cells.

Post Layout Simulation: check to see still the design still works.

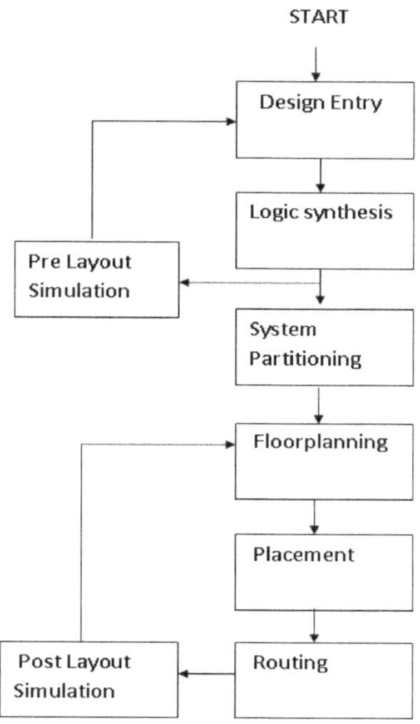

Figure 5.6: ASIC Design Flow

ASIC Design Advantages

- **Lower unit costs:** For very high volume designs costs comes out to be very less. A larger volume of ASIC design proves to be cheaper than implementing design using FPGA.

- **High speed:** ASIC gives design flexibility. This gives enormous opportunity for speed optimizations.

- **Low power:** ASIC can be optimized for required low power. There are several low power techniques such as power gating, clock gating, multi Vt cell libraries, pipelining etc are available to achieve the power target. Analog circuits and mixed signal designs can be implemented in ASIC. This is generally not possible in FPGA.

ASIC Design Disadvantages

- **Time-to-market:** Some large ASICs can take year of more to design. A good way to shorten development time is to make prototypes using FPGAs and then switch to an ASIC.

- **Design issues:** In ASIC we should take care of signal integrity issues and may more.

5.7. Programmable Logic Design

5.7.1. Array-based PLD

Programmable logic devices are available in standard configurations. It may be configured or programmed to create a designs customized to a specific applications.

1. PLA

It implements Boolean logic function. Both AND and OR planes are programmable. This approach allows for the implementation of arbitrary logic function in a two level Sum of Product form.

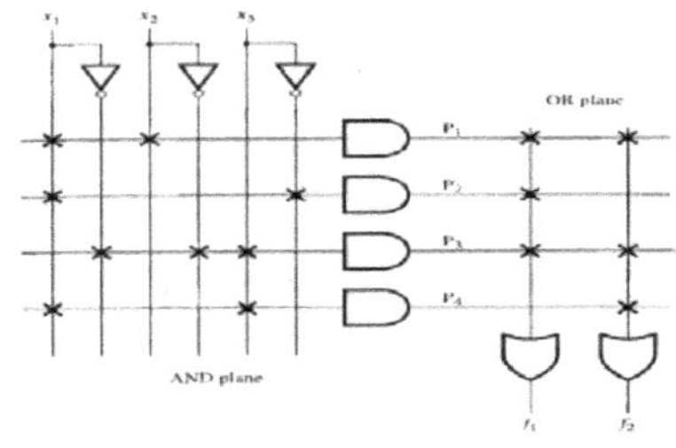

Figure 5.7: Implementation of Function Using PLA

Advantages of PLA

1. The structure is very regular which makes the estimation of parasitic easy. It enables accurate predictions of Area, speed and power dissipation.
2. It provides an efficient implementation of two level description of logic function.

2. PAL

In PAL OR plane is fixed and the AND plane is programmable.

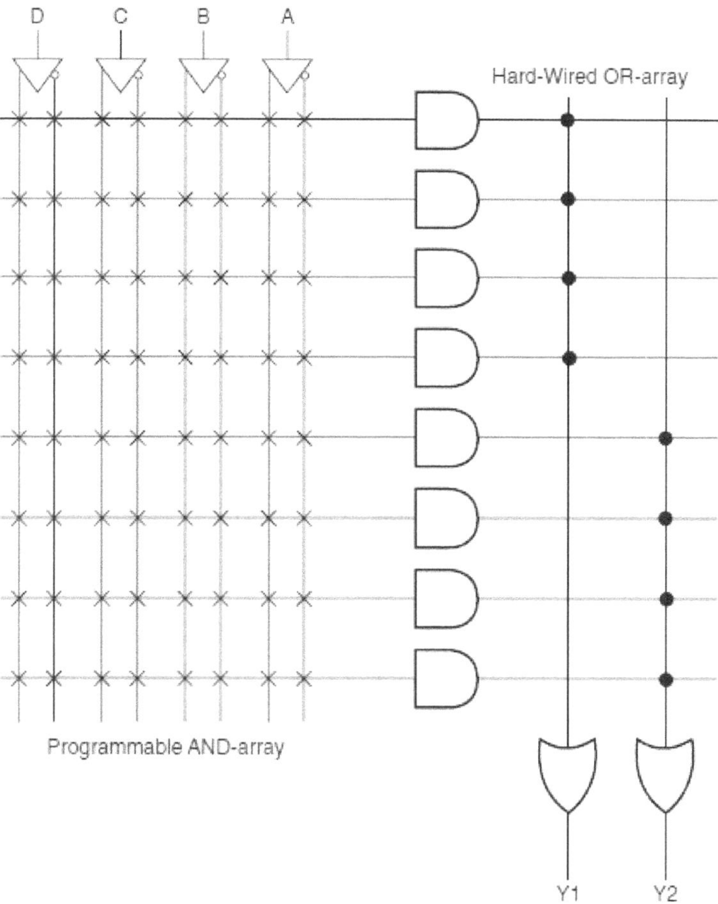

Figure 5.8: Implementation of Function Using PAL

3. Prom

In PROM AND plane is fixed and OR array is programmable. The sum of product approach results in regular structure and is very effective for logic functions that have a large fan in such as finite state machine. It is not effective for multilevel logic implementation.

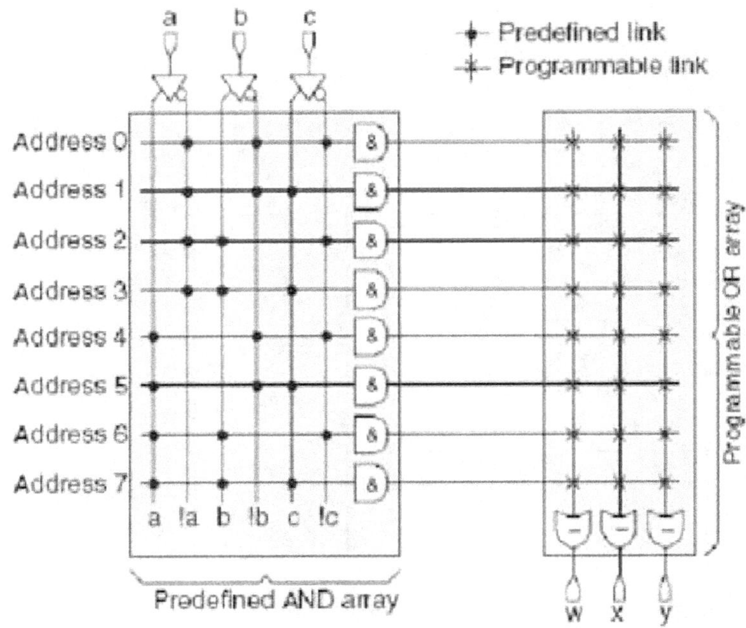

Figure 5.9: Implementation of Function Using PROM

5.8. Architecture of Field-Programmable Gate Array

An FPGA logic block is typically capable of implementing many different combinational and sequential logic functions. Current commercial FPGAs employ logic blocks that are based on one or more of the following:

- Transistor pairs.
- Basic small gates such as two-input NAND's or exclusive-OR's.
- Multiplexers.
- Look-up tables (LUT's).
- Wide fan-in AND-OR structures.

The Xilinx Logic Block

The basis for the Xilinx logic block is an SRAM functioning as a look-up table (LUT). The truth table for a K-input logic function is stored in a 2^k x 1 SRAM. The address lines of the SRAM function as inputs and the output of the SRAM provides the value of the logic function. If this logic function is implemented using a three-input LUT, then the SRAM would have a 1 stored at address 000, a 0 at 001 and so on, as specified by the truth table.

The advantage of look-up tables is that they exhibit high functionality. The disadvantages is that they are unacceptably large for more that about five inputs, since the number of memory cells needed for a K-input lookup table is 2^k.

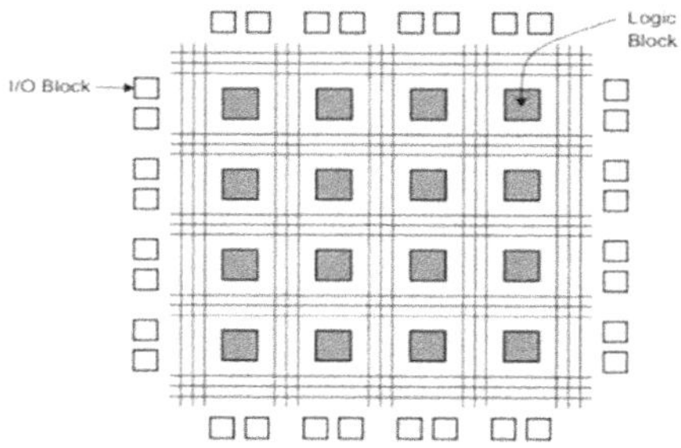

Figure 5.10: Basic Structure of FPGA

Xilinx 3000

The Xilinx 3000 series logic block contains a five-input one-output LUT. This block can be reconfigured into two four-input LUTs, with the constraint that together they use a total of no more than five distinct inputs. This reconfigurability provides flexibility that translates into better logic block utilization because many common logic functions do not require as many as five inputs. The block also contains sequential logic and several multiplexers that connect the combinational inputs and outputs to the flip-flops or outputs. These multiplexers are controlled by the SRAM cells that are loaded at programming time.

Xilinx 4000

The Xilinx 4000 series logic block contains two four-input LUT's feeding into a three-input LUT. In this block, all of the inputs are distinct and available external to the logic block. This block introduces two significant architectural changes from the 3000 series block. The architectural change in the Xilinx 4000 logic block is the use of two nonprogrammable connections from the two four-input LUT's to the three-input LUT. These connections are significantly faster than any programmable interconnection since no programmable switches are used in series, and little is present in parallel. If proper use can be made of these fast connections, FPGA performance can be greatly improved. The Xilinx 4000 block incorporate several additional features. Each LUT can be used directly as an SRAM block. This allows small amount of memory to be more efficiently implemented. Another feature is the inclusion of circuitry that can be used to implement fast carry addition circuits.

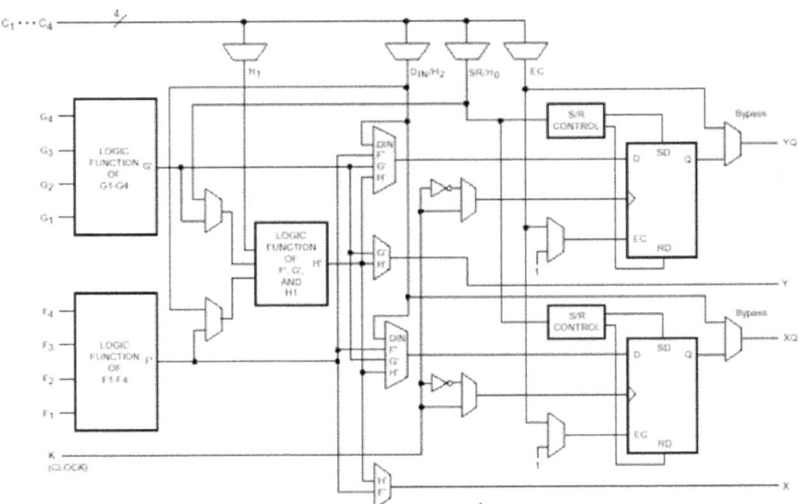

Figure 5.11: Block Diagram of XC 4000 Series

XC 5200 Logic Block

The basic logic cell used in XC5200is similar to CLBs used in the XC2000/3000/4000 CLBs but simpler. The XC 5200 basic logic cell (LC) contains a four input LUT, a flip flop and MUX to handle signal switching. The arithmetic carry logic is separate from the LUTs. Facility is available to connect parallel two LCs to form five input LUT.

Altera Logic Block

Altera FLEX

The basic logic cell is called logic element (LE).The FLEX LE uses a four input LUT, a flip flop, cascade logic and carry logic. Eight LEs are stacked to form a logic array block.

5.9.   Programmable Interconnect

Interconnect Network in FPGA is flexible. The interconnection between the gates must be programmable. Speed is the important parameter to be considered, because interconnect delay tends to dominate the performance. Interconnect does not consumes large power.

Xilinx EPLD

The XILINX EPLD family uses an interconnect bus known as universal Interconnection module (UIM) to distribute signals with in FPGA. It uses programmable AND array with constant delay from any input to each FB.

Altera MAX 5000 and 7000

Altera MAX 5000 and 7000 devices use a programmable Interconnect array (PIA).The PIA is a cross point switch for logic signals traveling between LABs. The advantage of this architecture is the fixed routing delay ie the delay between LAB1 and LAB2 is same as the distance LAB1 and LAB2. The size of the LAB array varies from devices to devices. MAX 9000 is an extremely coarse-grained Architecture.

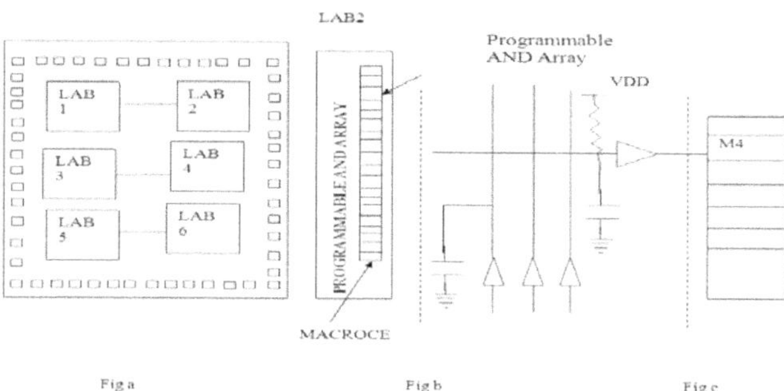

(a) The PIA (Programmable Interconnect Array) Deterministic-delay is Independent of the path length. (b) Each LAB (Logic Array Block) contains a programmable AND array. (c) Interconnect timing within a LAB is also fixed.

Figure 5.12: Simplified Block Diagram of the Altera MAX Interconnect Scheme

Altera FLEX

Altera FLEX is of finer grain than the MAX arrays because of the difference in programming technology. FLEX horizontal interconnect is much denser (168 channels per row). The Altera MAX 5000 series uses floating gate transistor-based programmable switch. Vertical wire passing by an AND gate can be connected as an input to the gate. The three product terms are the OR's together and can be inverted by an exclusive OR gate, which can also be used to implement other arithmetic functions. Notice that each input signal is provided in both true and complement form, with two separate wires. This programmable inversion significantly increases the functional capability of the block.

It is difficult, however, to make efficient use of all of the input to all of the gates, resulting in loss of density. This loss is not as severe as it first appears because of the high packing density of the wire-AND gates, as well as the fact that logic connections also serve as the routing function.

Programming Techniques

Several different programming techniques are used to implement the programmable switches. There are three types of such programmable switch technologies currently in use. These are:

- SRAM, where the switch is a pass transistor controlled by the state of SRAM bit.
- Antifuse which when electrically programmed, forms a low resistance path and
- EPROM, where the switch is a floating-gate transistor that can be turned off by injecting charge onto their floating gate.

An FPGA is programmed using electrically programmable switches. The properties of these programmable switches such as size, on-resistance, and capacitance may be of the tradeoffs in FPGA architecture..

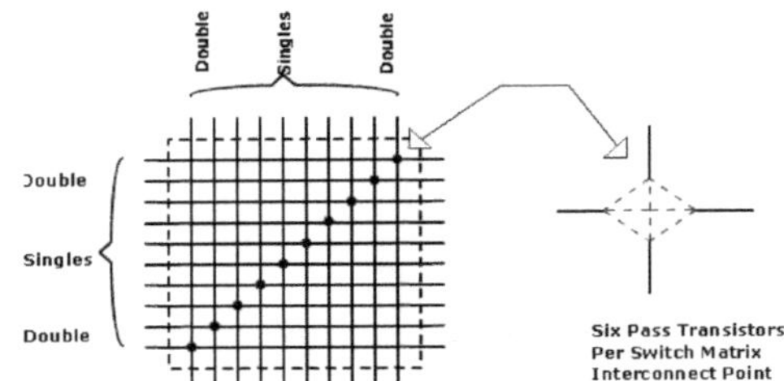

Figure 5.13: Programmable Switch Matrix

A. SRAM Programming Technology

The SRAM programming technology use Static RAM cells to control pass gates or multiplexers When a one is stored in the SRAM cell, the pass gate acts as a closed switch, and can be used to make a connection between two wire segments. When a zero is stored, the switch is open and the transistor presents a high resistance between the two wire segments.

For the multiplexer, the state of the SRAM cells connected to the select lines controls which one of the multiplexer inputs are connected to the output, as shown in Fig.

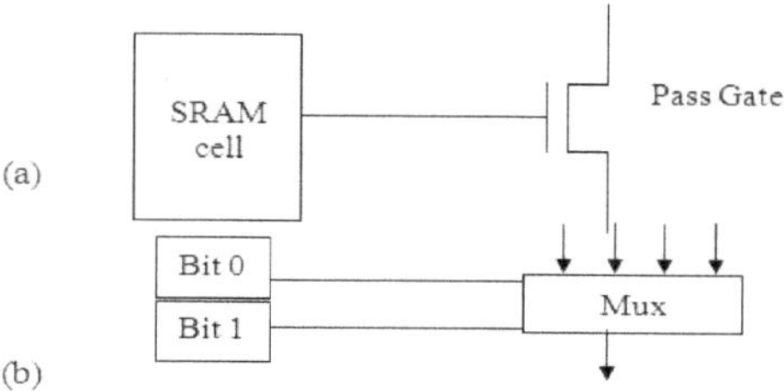

Figure 5.14: SRAM Programming

Since SRAM is volatile, the FPGA must be loaded and configured at the time of chip power-up. This requires external permanent memory to provide the programming bits such as PROM, EPROM, EEPROM or magnetic disk.

A major disadvantage of SRAM programming technology is its large area. It takes at least five transistors to implement an SRAM cell, plus at least one transistor to serve as a programmable switch. However, SRAM programming technology has two major advantages; fast re-programmability and it requires only standard integrated circuit process technology.

B. *Antifuse Programming Technology*

An antifuse is a two terminal device with an un-programmed state presenting a very high resistance between its terminals. When a high voltage (from 11 to 20 volts, depending on the type of antifuse) is applied across its terminals the antifuse will "blow" and create a low-resistance link. This link is permanent. Antifuse in use today are build either using an oxygen-nitrogen-oxygen (ONO) dielectric between N+ diffusion and polysilicon-silicon or amorphous silicon between metal layers or between polysilicon- silicon and the first layer of metal .

Programming an antifuse requires extra circuitry to deliver the high programming voltage and a relatively high current of 5 mA or more. This is done through fairly sizable pass transistors to provide addressing to each antifuse. A major advantage of the antifuse is its small size, little more than the cross-section of two metal wires. This advantage is somewhat reduced by the large size of the necessary programming transistors, which must be able to handle large currents, and the inclusion of isolation transistors that are sometimes needed to protect low voltage transistors from high programming voltages. A second major advantage of an antifuse is its relatively low series resistance.

C. Floating Gate Programming Technology

The floating gate programming technology uses technology found in ultraviolet erasable EPROM and electrically erasable EEPROM devices. The EPROM-based approach is used in Altera devices .The programmable switch is a transistor that can be permanently "disabled". This is accomplished by injecting a charge on the floating gate using a high voltage between the control gate 1 and the drain of the transistor. This charge increases the threshold voltage of the transistor so that it turns off. The charge is removed by exposing the floating gate to UV light. This lowers the threshold voltage of the transistor and makes the transistor function normally.

Rather than using an EPROM transistor directly as a programmable switch, the unprogrammed transistor is used to pull down a "bit line" when the "word line" is set high.This approach can be used to implement a wired-AND style of logic, thereby providing both logic and routing.

When compared with SRAM programming technology, a major advantage of the EPROM technology is its re-programmability and no external permanent memory is needed to program the chip on power-up. EPROM technology, however, requires three additional processing steps over an ordinary CMOS process. Two other disadvantages are the high ON-resistance of an EPROM transistor and the high static power consumption due to the pull-up resistance used.

5.10. Routing Architecture

The routing architecture of an FPGA is the manner in which the programmable switches and wiring segments are positioned to allow the programmable interconnection of the logic blocks. A wire segment is a wire unbroken by programmable switches. One or more switches may attach to the wire segment. Each end of a wire segment typically has a switch attached. A track is a sequence of one or more wire segments in a line. A routing channel is a group of parallel tracks.

A connection block provides connectivity from the inputs and outputs of a logic block to the wire segments in the channels. There can be connection blocks in the vertical direction as well as in the horizontal direction. The second structure is the switch block, which provides connectivity between the horizontal as well as vertical wire segments. The switch block provides connectivity among the wire segments incident to its four sides. In some architecture, the switch block and connection block are intermingled, and in others they are combined into a single structure.

Routing is made simple by first global routing followed by detailed routing. The input to the global router is a floorplan that includes the location of all the fixed blocks and the placement information for flexible blocks. A global router does not make any interconnections. It just plans the connections

The objective of the global routing are:

1. Minimize the total interconnect length.
2. Maximize the probability that the detailed router can complete the routing.
3. Minimize the critical path delay.

1. *The Xilinx Routing Architecture*

The routing architecture used in the Xilinx 3000 series FPGA connects the logic block into the channel through a connection block. Since each connection site is large because of the SRAM programming technology, the Xilinx 3000 connection block typically connects each pin to only two or three out of the five tracks passing by a block. On all four sides of the logic block are implemented with pass transistors for the output pins and multiplexers for the input pins. The use of multiplexers reduces the number of SRAM cells needed per pin. Once the logic block pin is connected via the connection block, the switch block makes connections between segments in intersecting horizontal and vertical channels. As the expanded picture in the lower right-hand corner shows, each wire segment can connect to a subject of the wire segments on opposing sides of the block. Each wire segment can typically connect to five or six out of a possible 15 wire segments on the opposing sides. Again, this number is limited by the large size and capacities of the SRAM programmable switches. There are four types of wire segments provided in the Xilinx 3000 architecture:

- General-purpose interconnect consisting of wire segments that pass through switches in the switch block.
- Direct interconnect consisting of wire segments that connect each logic block output directly to four nearest neighbors as illustrated by the thick black lines emanating from the corner block
- Long lines, which span the length of width of the chip, providing high-fanout uniform delay connections, indicated by the dashed lines in
- A clock line which is a single net that spans the entire chip and is driven by a high-drive buffer. This line is connected only to the clock input of the flip-flops, and provides for a low-skew clocking scheme.

The routing architecture of an FPGA could be as simple as a nearest neighbor mesh or as complex as the perfect shuffle used in multiprocessors. More typically, an FPGA routing architecture incorporates wire segments of varying lengths which can be interconnected via electricity programmable switches. The choice of the number of wire segments incorporated affects the density achieved by an FPGA. If an inadequate number of segments is used, only a small fraction of the logic blocks can be utilized, resulting in poor FPGA density; conversely the use of an excess number of segments that go unused also wastes area.

The distribution of the lengths of the wire segments also greatly affects the density and performance achieved by an FPGA. For example, if all segments are chosen to be long, implementing local interconnection becomes too costly in area and delay. On the other hand if all segments are short, long interconnections are implemented using too many switches in series, resulting in unacceptably large delays.

5.11. Types of Global Routing

Sequential routing and Hierarchical routing are the two methods of Global routing.

5.11.1. Sequential Routing

It takes each net and calculates the shortest path using tree or graph algorithm. Sequential routing uses order-Independent or order-dependent method. In order-independent method the channel assignment will be the same whether a particular net is processed first or last. Order-dependent method is sequential. Here a global router can consider the number of interconnects placed already in various channel.

5.11.2. Hierarchical Routing

Rather than handling all the nets on the chip at the same time, the global routing problem is simplified by dividing the chip area in to levels of Hierarchy.

5.12. Detailed Routing

The objective of detailed routing are to minimize one or more of the:
1. The total interconnects length and area.
2. The number of layer changes.
3. The delay of critical path.

The global router determines the channels to be used for each interconnect. With the knowledge of this information, the detailed router decides the exact location of and layers of interconnect. Left Edge and Maze running algorithms are used for detailed routing.

1. Give the difference between CPLD & FPGA.

Both CPLD and FPGA fall under the category of Programmable Logic Devices. CPLD comprises multiple circuit blocks (which are PLA or PAL like) on a single chip with internal wiring resources to connect the circuit blocks. Each PAL like block is connected to a circuit labeled I/O block which is attached to a number of the chips input and output pins.

FPGA is a PLD that supports implementation of relatively large logic circuits. They provide logic blocks for implementation of the required functions. FPGA has 3 types of resources, namely, logic blocks, I/O blocks for connecting to the pins of the package, and interconnection wires and switches.

2. Why is PLDs popular compared to ASICs.

PLDs have a very general structure and include a collection of programmable switches that allow the internal circuitry in the chip to be configured in many different ways. These switches are programmed by the end user, rather than when the chip is manufactured. ASIC is a chip designed from scratch. The logic circuitry that must be included on the chip is designed first and then an appropriate technology is chosen to implement the chip. Then the chip is manufactured by a company that has the fabrication facilities. This process is time consuming and can be cost effective only in a bulk demand situation. Due to these reasons, PLDs are more popular than ASICs.

3. List the basic steps in designing with an LCA.
   1. Design a system using gates and flip-flops
   2. Enter a logic diagram of the system into the computer using a schematic capture program.
   3. Run an automatic place and route program which greaks the logic diagram into pieces which will fit into the configurable logic blocks. Place them in appropriate places in the LCA and then route the interconnections between the logic blocks.
   4. Run a program which will generate the bit pattern necessary to program the LCA.
   5. Download the bit pattern into the internal RAM memory cells in the LCA and test the operation of the LCA.

4. Differentiate between PAL & PLA.

Both PAL and PLA uses AND-OR arrays. PAL has a programmable AND array and a fixed OR array. Whereas PLA has both AND and OR array programmable.

5. What is a LUT?

Look up Table is a memory organization through which a cell's combinational logic may be physically implemented. LUT devices are more flexible and provide more inputs per cell but at the expense of propagation delay.

6. What is the function of a placement CAD tool?

Placement CAD tool determines where in the target device each logic function in the optimized circuit will be realized. Placement task highly depends on the implementation technology.

7. What is meant by routing? What are its different phases?

After the placement of logic functions in macro cells wires in the chip are to be used to realize the required interconnections. This step is called routing. It is performed in 2 phases, Global routing and local routing. A good routing algorithm will attempt to minimize the total routing area.

8. What is a boundary scan test?

Boundary scan test is a method for testing boards and ASICs using a four-wire interface.

9. How is boundary scan test performed on a PCB or ASIC?

To detect failures, manufacturers use boundary scan to test every connection between ASICs on a board. During boundary scan, test data is loaded into each ASIC and then driven on to the board traces. Each ASIC monitor their input, captures the data received and then shifts the captured data out. Any defect in the board or ASIC connections will show up as a discrepancy between expected and actual measured continuity data

10. Mention the important building blocks of an FPGA

Important building blocks in FPGA are

1. Logic block.
2. I/O block.
3. Interconnect switches and wires.

11. Mention the important building blocks of an CPLD.

1. I/O block.
2. Switch matrix.
3. Function block.
4. In-system programming controller.

12. What is done in synthesis process?

It is the process of conversion of HDL code to gate level net list of the design. Net list is the connectivity description of gate level circuit. Synthesis is a target technology dependent issue, so user has to specify the target /device correctly including its package type and speed grade. After synthesis, EDA tool will generate EDIF/XNF file.

13. What is meant by in - system programming?

Instead of relying on a programming unit to configure a chip, the chip can be made to program on the circuit board itself. This method is called In System Programming. The circuitry which allows ISP is standardized by IEEE and is called JTAG (Joint Test Action Group) port.

14. Name the various building blocks of an FPGA.

Configurable logic blocks (CLB), Input/output Block (IOB) and Switch Matrix (Interconnects)

15. What is a CPLD?

CPLD stands for Complex Programmable Logic Device. They can be programmed as per the user's logic and can perform the user application.

They are reprogrammable and the design modification is easy. CPLD consists of multiple circuit blocks on a single chip, with internal wiring resources to connect the circuit blocks. Each circuit block is a PLA or PAL like blocks.

16. List two advantages & two disadvantages of FPGA based design. Advantages:
    1. Supports implementation of relatively large logic circuits.
    2. It can be configured in many different ways.

Disadvantages

    1. Storage cells in FPGA are volatile.
    2. Limited utilization of cells based on application.
17. What are the benefits of implementing combinational logic functions using PLAs when compared with ROMs?

Advantageous of PLA Approach

    1. Design tools are available for multi-output minimization.
    2. There are relatively few unique minterm combinations.
    3. Many minterms are shared among the output functions.

Disadvantages of ROM

1. Size doubles for each additional input.
2. Can't exploit don't cares.

18. What are the advantages of PLA?

1. Can be programmed outside of the manufacturing environment
2. Most programmable logic devices are erasable and reprogrammable.
3. Allows "updating" a device or correction of errors
4. Allows reuse the device for a different design
5. Ideal for course laboratories
6. Programmable logic devices can be used to prototype design that will be implemented for sale in regular ICs.

Question Bank

Part-A

1. Give the constituent of I/O cell in 22V10.

2. What is a FPGA?

3. What are the different methods of programming of PALs

4. What is an antifuse?

5. What are the different levels of design abstraction at physical design?

6. What are macros?

7. What is Programmable Interconnects?

8. Give the steps in ASIC design flow.

9. Give the Xilinx configurable logic block.

10. Give the XILINX FPGA architecture

11. Differentiate between channeled & channel less gate array

12. Explain the ASIC design flow with a neat diagram

Part–B

1. Explain the general architecture of FPGA and bring about different programmable blocks used.

2. Discuss in detail about full custom design and semi custom design.

3. Describe about Gate-Array Based ASICs.

4. Write short note on programmable Logic Devices.

5. Write short notes on standard cell design and cell libraries.

6. Write the significance of PLA in VLSI design.

7. Explain the programmable interconnects and I/O blocks used in FPGA.

B.E/B.Tech Degree Examination

Sixth Semester

Medical Electronics

(Common to Electronics and Communication Engineering)

May/June 2016

VLSI Design

Regulation 2013

Part-A

Answer all Questions   **10*2=20 marks**

1. State channel length modulation. Write down the equation for describing the channel length modulation effect in NMOS transistor.
2. What is latch-up? How to prevent latch-up.
3. Give Elmore delay expression for propagation delay of an inverter.
4. Why single phase dynamic logic structure cannot be cascaded? Justify.
5. Draw the switch level schematic of multiplexer based NMOS latch using NMOS only pass transistor for multiplexers.
6. What is clocked CMOS register?
7. What is meant by bit sliced data path organization?
8. Determine the propagation delay of n bit carry select adder.
9. What are feed through cells? State their uses.
10. State the features of full custom design.

Part-B

11. A)
(i) Describe the equation for source to drain current in the three regions of operation of a MOS transistor and draw the VI Characteristics.   (8)
(ii) Explain in detail about the body effect and its effect in MOS device.

OR

B)

(i) Explain the DC transfer characteristics of a CMOS Inverter with necessary conditions for the different regions of operation.

12. A)

(a) Draw the static CMOS logic circuit for the following expression.

    a) $Y = \overline{A.B.C.D}$

    b) $Y = \overline{D(A+BC)}$

(b) Discuss in detail the characteristics of CMOS Transmission gate.

OR

B) What are the sources of power dissipation in CMOS and discuss various design techniques to reduce power dissipation in CMOS?

13. A) Explain the operation of master-slave based edge triggered register.

OR

B) Discuss in detail the various pipelining approaches to optimize sequential logic circuits.

14. A) Design a 16 bit carry bypass and carry select adder and discuss their features.

OR

B) Design a 4*4 array multiplier and write down the equation for delay.

15. A) With neat sketch explain the CLB, IOB and programmable interconnects of an FPGA device.

OR

B) Write brief notes on

    (i) Full custom ASIC.

    (ii) Semi custom ASIC.

B.E/B.Tech Degree Examination

Sixth Semester

Medical Electronics

(Common to Electronics and Communication engineering)

Nov/ Dec 2016

VLSI Design

Regulation 2013

Part-A

1. Define body bias effect.
2. Draw the stick diagram and layout for CMOS Inverter.
3. What I s the value of V_{out} for the figure shown below, where V_{tn} is threshold voltage of transistor?

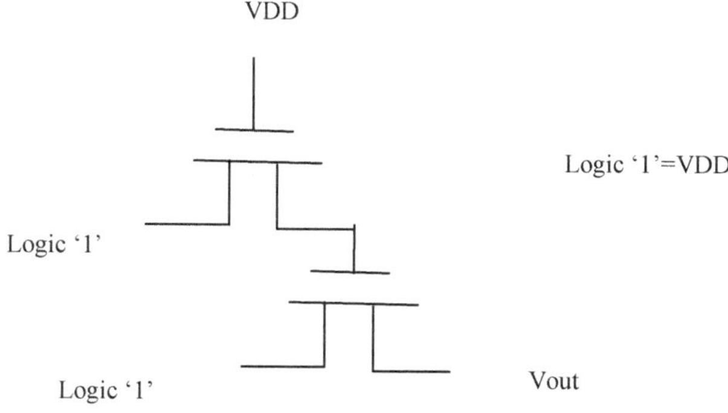

4. List out the sources of static and dynamic power dissipation
5. What is meant by pipelining?
6. Draw the schematic of dynamic edge- triggered register.
7. Why is barrel shifter very useful in the designing of arithmetic circuiots?
8. Write the principle of any one fast multiplier?
9. What is the standard cell based ASIC design?
10. What is an antifuse? State its merits and demerits.

Part-B

11. A)

   (i) Explain the different steps involved in N-Well fabrication process with neat diagram.

                          (12)

   (ii) Derive the noise margin for a CMOS inverter.

OR

B)

   (i) Discuss in detail with a neat layout the design rules for a CMOS inverter.

   (ii) Discuss the mathematical equations that can be used to model the drain current and diffusion capacitance of MOS transistor.

12. A) Write short notes on:

   (i) Ratioed Circuits.

   (ii) Dynamic CMOS circuits.

OR

B)

   (i) Estimate least delay and determine input capacitance of each stages for the logic network shown in figure, which may represent the critical path of a more complex logic block. The output of the network is loaded with a capacitance which is 5 times larger than the input capacitance of the first gate, which is minimum sized inverter.

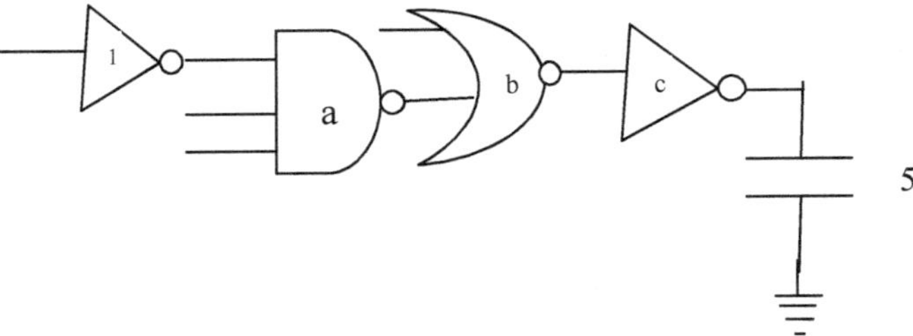

   (ii) Explain the dynamic power dissipation in CMOS circuits with necessary diagrams and expressions.

13. A) Discuss in detail the various static latches and registers

OR

B) Write short notes on:

     (i) True single phase clocked register.

     (ii) NORA-CMOS latches.

14.

    (i) Explain the operation of a basic 4 bit adder. Describe the different approaches of improving the speed of the adder.

OR

    (ii) Explain the operation of booth multiplication with suitable examples? Justify how booths algorithm speed up the multiplication process.

15.

    (i) Discuss the different types of programming Technology used in FPGA design.

OR

    (ii) Briefly explain the semicustom ASIC with its characteristics.